THE SOUL OF
HUMANITY

Wisdom
Editions

Minneapolis

First Edition September 2023

The Soul of Humanity: How rational thinking can save us from the chaos of blind faith. Copyright © 2023 by Massoud Kazemzadeh and Gary Lindberg. All rights reserved.

10 9 8 7 6 5 4 3 2 1

ISBN: 978-1-960250-94-0

Cover and book design by Gary Lindberg

The symbols on the back cover represent eight of the world's great wisdom traditions. From the top down, these are the Bahá'í Faith, the Bábí Faith, Islam, Christianity, Zoroastrianism, Buddhism, Judaism and Hinduism.

The front cover image is a creative rendering of *The Thinker*, a bronze sculpture by Auguste Rodin in the Musée Rodin, Paris.

THE SOUL OF HUMANITY

How rational thinking can save us
from the chaos of blind faith

MASSOUD KAZEMZADEH
GARY LINDBERG

Wisdom
Editions

Minneapolis

God's greatest gift to man is that of intellect, or understanding.
The understanding is the power by which man acquires his knowledge
of the several kingdoms of creation, and of various stages of existence,
as well as of much which is invisible.

– 'Abdu'l-Bahá, *Paris Talks*

Table of Contents

To all humanity without distinction or conditions

Chapter 1:
The Slow Maturity of Humanity

The yearning for belief is inextinguishable, an inherent part of what makes one human.[1]

Right now, nearly a quarter of the way into the twenty-first century, world leaders of all stripes appear to have learned very little from history and philosophy. As has nearly always been the case, it is easy to imagine that we are headed for some kind of Armageddon. Over recent centuries and in blind pursuit of wealth, we have despoiled our environment, and opinions regarding how to handle the environmental crisis have grown toxic; increasingly dangerous wars, bloody and inhuman as always, threaten to lead into nuclear conflict, which could end humanity faster than global warming; a greater divide between the poorest of us and the richest is causing even greater struggles for the vast majority; the advent of social media, a brilliant invention for democratizing and enhancing communications, has led to a new barbarism in which the same old power struggle exists between lies and truth. The domination of propaganda and erosion of civility threaten to destroy us sooner than any war or overheating of the planet.

As if our short-term view were not amply depressing, if we were to project our destination on our present course a thousand years from now—as we should—where would we be? Would we still

---

1   *Century of Light*, commissioned by the Universal House of Justice, p. 60

be here, or would Earth's ability to support us have collapsed under our lack of stewardship? Would society have advanced toward peace or more devasting conflict? Would we have come together as a truly harmonious society embracing its diversity or perhaps have lapsed into hyper-tribalism like our primitive ancestors?

Fortunately, the optimistic view is within reach. This view recognizes that even though our history on Earth has been dysfunctional and unforgiving, humankind has found ways of slowly and grudgingly organizing itself into communities and establishing a semblance of order that has allowed individuals—as they became free from the overwhelming burden of pure survival—to *think*—yes, to think, which has helped them to start making sense out of the world in which they lived. By thinking rationally, they found that rules of conduct were necessary to govern societies and that certain kinds of conduct were generally good for everyone, and other behaviors were bad.

Lacking scientific knowledge but possessing a degree of creativity—a hallmark of humans—early attempts to make sense of the world produced a variety of superstitions and pantheons of gods to explain the observable phenomena around them. These unfounded beliefs became the bedrock on which entire cultures were built and to which countless individuals passionately declared allegiance. Despite this, humankind—through the power of rational thinking and insights gained from a divine source—began to discern scientific facts from the mire of superstition and tradition. Wars still raged, and cities remained walled up to defend against neighboring societies, but despite an ever-advancing civilization fueled by rational minds these older ways of thinking and behaving persist even today.

The authors suggest that in our present, despite our seemingly endless global issues and petty disputes, human society metaphorically has entered its adolescence. Still plagued by a degree of immaturity and certain playground bullies, humanity has developed to a point where its capacity for accomplishment has been heightened, but its accomplishments are still blunted by irrational childlike tendencies.

Our young people have been rapidly turning away from religion, which they see as irrelevant and not rational.

> Humanity is now experiencing the commotions invariably associated with the most turbulent stage of its evolution, the stage of adolescence, when the impetuosity of youth and its vehemence reach their climax, and must gradually be superseded by the calmness, the wisdom, and the maturity that characterize the stage of manhood.[2]

If the desired result of our collective lives is to establish universal peace and prosperity for all humankind now and forever—quite a tall order—then perhaps we should accelerate our development by making better decisions for all of humanity.

> ...[The] challenge to all people, believers and unbelievers, clergy and laymen alike, is to recognize the consequences now being visited upon the world as the result of the universal corruption of the religious impulse. In the prevailing alienation of humanity from God over the past century, a relationship on which the fabric of moral life itself depends has broken down.[3]

Are we on the right course to help the next generation thrive? There are many questions that affect the whole of humanity and not just one ethnic group, one nation or one religious or political community. Each of them requires us to make important decisions. Unfortunately, most of us have been mentally conditioned to reach conclusions in one of two ways: through rational thinking or by blind faith.

---

2   Shoghi Effendi, *The World Order of Bahá'u'lláh*, p. 202
3   "A Statement on Baha'u'llah" by the Bahá'í International Community, Chapter 11.

3

In this book, we challenge the use of blind faith to reach conclusions. Moving forward, we will argue in favor of the need to evaluate—in many cases, to *reevaluate*—all aspects of our social, political, financial and religious lives through rational analysis, which means abandoning decisions and conclusions based on blind faith. It seems clear today that evidence-based thinking, which we call rational thinking, is a prerequisite for unifying humanity, something which we will discuss later.

The aim of this book is not to disparage or discredit any religious beliefs of the past, but simply to examine such beliefs through the lens of rational or reasonable thinking. Behind every belief is a history, and all beliefs—including the human behaviors they foster—are influenced by their origins. We have cited quotations from various Holy Scriptures, particularly from Judaism, Christianity, Islam and the Bahá'í Faith. It is up to the reader to reflect on these Writings.

Rational thinking is available to all who are not held captive by blind faith in cherished beliefs. Rational thought allows us to have intelligent conversations with others about important issues without the intrusion of hurtful emotional outbursts. On the other hand, blind faith, which is not grounded in facts or logic, is valuable only for the individual who possesses it and lacks meaning for others. Conclusions and personal views based on blind faith are ill-suited for social discourse and usually lead to disunity.

Here are some questions to help us examine our thinking:

- How are our decisions based on faith and influenced by religion, politics, prejudices and peer pressures, and how will they affect our future?

- Can we safeguard our shared home, planet Earth, if we do not make significant changes in our lifestyles, attitudes and cherished cultural beliefs, which have been passed down to us from our forebears?

- Can we give up old ways of thinking and decision-making, or are we doomed to blindly follow the traditions, folklore and beliefs of our ancestors?

- Will humanity destroy itself with new inventions, the uses of which are influenced by old ideas based on emotion and blind faith, or can unbiased reason create a new way of life?

- Could this new way of life also encompass a global reformation in religious, political, social and financial thought to affirm the fundamental unity of all humanity, especially at a time when the loud, clashing narratives of conservatism and liberalism seek to obliterate all opposition?

- Can a new voice stand out against the white-washed extremism of both sides of the current political divide?

- Is there any hope that humanity is progressing both materially and rationally, and that the present time of tumultuous adolescence will soon develop into a period of maturity with a world-embracing vision?

A fundamental belief of the authors is this: The greatest truth emerging from recent history is that all humanity—the billions of us who share the joys and challenges of life on this planet—are like the members of one immense family. And as one family...

> The injury of one shall be considered the injury of all; the comfort of each, the comfort of all; the honor of one, the honor of all.[4]

How can humanity learn to appreciate the need for achieving unity and detach itself from the outdated cultural beliefs, traditions and rituals that have ultimately led us to disunity and deadly conflict? Understanding the historic origin of such beliefs and customs, and the role played by unthinking faith, is a first step.

---

4   'Abdu'l-Baha, *The Promulgation of Universal Peace*, p. 168.

Over millennia, advancements in technology and science have brought humanity into a new age that both fosters and requires advanced ways of thinking. Just as the meaning of words can change over time, so do concepts and mental processes. For example, today the popular use of the word "soul" can describe both the personal essence of an individual as well as the collective essence of humanity. For an individual, this essence or soul could be thought of as closely associated with a person's thoughts—which requires language engendered in the synaptic structure of the mind—not his or her material existence. It is one's thoughts that distinguish each person from another and elevate humans above the realm of the animal.

It is probably no accident that in the world's great religions the exercises for nurturing spirituality are often related to how we think. They ask us to discover truth for ourselves and adapt our thinking to it. It seems clear that gaining knowledge, which is the outcome of education, investigation and rational thought, is a worthwhile mission for every member of society and may be the gateway to that mysterious entity many people call the "soul."

Those who allow themselves to be governed by blind faith are often content with having no rational thoughts to disturb their faith. Thinking logically will naturally challenge blind faith. It requires gathering facts and then scrutinizing their sources and their veracity. Finding truth requires us to extract meaning and reach conclusions even when our conclusions contradict those of close friends and family members or defy our cultural traditions, conventional wisdom or recognized authorities.

If we don't have the time or energy to rationally analyze everything in our lives, then it makes sense to set priorities. If your priority is to understand your purpose in life and become the best human being you can be—in other words, to develop your capacity to help others and be a better spouse, parent, sibling, grandparent, aunt or uncle, friend or acquaintance—then this book will be useful for you. And you in turn may be more useful to your family and your society.

It starts with eliminating the kind of faith that is blind to reason—the kind that has infiltrated all aspects of society—and replacing it with a rational and personal search for truth. Once that manner of truth is found, it will provide a source of energy, certitude and guidance that can change everything.

Mahatma Gandhi said, "Faith… must be enforced by reason… when faith becomes blind it dies."[5] And as physicist Albert Einstein summarized, "The further the spiritual evolution of mankind advances, the more certain it seems to me that the path to genuine religiosity does not lie through the fear of life, and the fear of death, and blind faith, but through striving after rational knowledge."[6]

This book proposes that through such striving lies the most direct highway to the unification of humankind.

As we actively engage in this sense-making journey with minds uncluttered by the ghosts of old thinking, we are not alone. Wise sages or, as many believe, God or Prophets informed by God, have left breadcrumb trails of wisdom as signposts. Most people refer to these traditions as religions such as Hinduism, Buddhism, Judaism, Christianity, Islam and the Baha'í Faith. In his masterwork entitled The author prefer to call them "wisdom traditions," which emphasizes the wisdom they imparted, and still impart, to society in general.

For centuries, a person's "religion" has been a way to easily identify enemies—those who hold blasphemous beliefs contrary to our own, worship false gods and perform nonsensical or offensive rituals. This work takes the position, that rather than being isolated belief systems created or plagiarized by corrupt or misguided individuals, these "wisdom traditions" each have an uncorrupted essence that is true and mysteriously connected, and each is part of an unfolding body of knowledge.

---

5   *The Wit and Wisdom of Gandhi* (ed. 1951)

6   https://libquotes.com/search/?q=The+further+the+spiritual+evolution+of+mankind+advances

A deep study of the teachings of these wisdom traditions reveals that their spiritual principles are fundamentally the same. Whenever similarities exist where they should not, researchers often reasonably speculate that some unknown source of information or guidance was behind the similarities. The existence of pyramid-shaped structures in such far-flung countries as Egypt, Central and South America, and even China, have sent archaeologists searching for signs of contact between these ancient civilizations, so far without success.

Most of the wisdom traditions we think of as religions give credit to a common source, a supreme being called by different names in various languages. The human prophet-founder of each tradition claimed that authority and knowledge was conferred upon Him by this supreme being and set out to educate humankind with this knowledge becoming, in essence, a "Divine Educator." The knowledge possessed by each of these Educators had to be revealed in lessons appropriate to the capacity of the current society to understand it, otherwise it would be misunderstood or dismissed as meaningless. In other words, Abraham could not address the need for global unity to a tribal society that could barely envision life beyond the visible horizon. But lessons delivered later to more advanced societies could be understood. According to this concept, "religions" are not necessarily separate and competing philosophies but one unfolding religion of God. Over thousands of years, civilization has been continuously educated as if moving through different grades in school. One cannot learn calculus in first grade. As the capacity of the student increases with maturity and an understanding of fundamental principles, more advanced concepts can be learned.

In addition, humankind has profited greatly from great thinkers and scientists, who through rational exploration have challenged faith-based beliefs and the concomitant status quo, thereby contributing to the advancement of humanity, albeit incrementally.

A basic premise of this book is captured in the following passage, which we will try to prove is the true explanation of human capacity:

> The human spirit which distinguishes man from the animal is the rational soul, and these two names—the human spirit and the rational soul—designate one thing. This spirit, which... is called the rational soul, encompasses all things and as far as human capacity permits, discovers their realities and becomes aware of the properties and effects, the characteristics and conditions of earthly things. But the human spirit, unless it be assisted by the spirit of faith, cannot become acquainted with the divine mysteries and the heavenly realities. It is like a mirror which, although clear, bright, and polished, is still in need of light. Not until a sunbeam falls upon it can it discover the divine mysteries. As for the mind, it is the power of the human spirit. The spirit is as the lamp, and the mind as the light that shines from it. The spirit is as the tree, and the mind as the fruit. The mind is the perfection of the spirit and a necessary attribute thereof, even as the rays of the sun are an essential requirement of the sun itself.[7]

We will discuss the provocative concept of the "progressive revelation" of logical truth later. What is relevant here is that the authors of this book have searched the various wisdom traditions for relevant clues that could help us construct a framework for a more comprehensive and rational understanding of this ever-unfolding knowledge. These clues are contained in quotations from the Scriptures of the various wisdom traditions. The authors believe that a rational and comprehensive plan for humanity emerges from a combination of ancient insights illuminated by the most recent wisdom traditions aimed at educating a contemporary society.

The reader's job will be to use rational thinking to draw meaningful conclusions. The authors expect readers to try to set aside prejudices, preconceived ideas and emotional responses and then consider if the

---

7   'Abdu'l-Bahá, *Some Answered Questions*, chapter 55.

content makes sense or not. If you disagree, we would like to hear from you at this email address: soul@calumeteditions.com.

Conventions Used in This Book

Capitalization

Throughout this book, the authors have chosen to capitalize words that refer to the Divine or the Revelation of the Divine, including pronouns. This practice honors the generally accepted conventions followed in many of the sacred Scriptures of the world's great wisdom traditions. Nevertheless, there are capitalization inconsistencies in quoted King James versions of various biblical passages. We have chosen to always use the capitalization originally used in Scriptural passages even when they are fossilized compared to modern usage.

Use of Masculine Gender

In many languages, the use of the masculine gender, unless intended specifically to denote masculinity, is generic. For instance, in English we speak of the race of man, or mankind, in both instances meaning every member of the human race—men, women and children. There would be no reason to interpret "O Son of Being," or "O Son of Man" as addressed only to males. It is the same with pronouns.

> The truth is that all mankind are the creatures and servants of one God, and in His estimate all are human. "Man" is a generic term applying to all humanity. The biblical statement "Let us make man in our image, after our likeness" does not mean that woman was not created. The image and likeness of God apply to her as well. In Persian and Arabic there are two distinct words translated into English as man: one meaning man and woman collectively, the other distinguishing man as male from woman the female. The first word and its pronoun are generic, collective; the other is restricted to the male.[8]

---

8 'Abdu'l-Bahá, *The Promulgation of Universal Peace: Talks Delivered by 'Abdu'l-Bahá during His Visit to the United States and Canada in 1912*, rev. ed. (Wilmette:

The problem of commonly used gender-specific nouns (chairman, postman) has two potential solutions. One is to change the usage of nouns; the other is to permit the consciousness of sexual equality to modify the meaning of nouns that were once standard usage. Undoubtedly, both courses will be followed in the evolution of English and other languages. The word "doctor," for example, is now clearly of common gender in English, although originally masculine. In specifically addressing this issue, the Bahá'í Faith issued the following statement:

> Our feeling is that, in general, it is preferable to permit the change of consciousness to change the meaning that people attribute to the words, rather than to press the use of forms of words that seem contrived and, to many people, ridiculous—a reaction that does not help the advancement of the cause of the equality of the sexes.[9]

The authors agree with this assessment and have chosen to ask readers of this to interpret masculine pronouns and nouns in quoted passages to explicitly apply to both males and females. In the fresh material written by the authors, however, an attempt has been made to avoid the issue by making inclusive word choices or including both gender-based pronouns. These language issues are not trivial, since language is our chief tool for communication with each other and bringing about the unity of humankind.

Diacritics

A diacritic is a mark near or through a written character or combination of characters indicating a phonetic value different from that given the unmarked or otherwise marked element. We often think of diacritics as accent marks or symbols above

---

Bahá'í Publishing Trust, 1995), pp. 174 and 374.
    9   November 1989, from a memorandum from the Universal House of Justice to the Bahá'í Office of Public Information.

or below letters (examples: Ḍ ẓ Á í Gh kh). Bahá'í Writings use a standard system of conventions used for writing a language to Romanize Persian and Arabic script. The system used in Bahá'í literature was set in 1923, and although it was based on a commonly used standard of the time, it has its own embellishments that make it unique. The authors have chosen to use Bahá'í diacritics when documenting names or words originating in the Persian or Arabic languages.

Quotations from Wisdom Traditions

Throughout this book, the authors refer to Writings from the world's great wisdom traditions, often considered as world religions. The intent of the authors is for these passages to be considered on their own merits as traditional wisdom, not because they may have been of divine origin. There is no intent to promote one of these religions over another; in fact, we believe an individual should study them all. The fact that there are a greater number of quotations from the Bahá'í Faith is due to the facts that older wisdom traditions spoke to less knowledgeable societies that lacked sophisticated scientific knowledge and thus seldom, if ever, commented on the modern issues this book addresses, and because civilization has progressed in all respects over time.

Design of Quotations

In this book, the designer has chosen to put all Scriptural quotations from all wisdom traditions in gray boxes. Quotes from secular authors are not in boxes.

Chapter 2:
The Realms of Existence

The Shared Experience of a Soul

Not everyone believes in the existence of a soul, but a vast majority of humanity expresses a powerful impression of its existence. This shared experience, which we see uncovered in the archeological discoveries of paleolithic through neolithic ritual sites, gives rise in early humankind to burials and funerary rights reflecting a belief in an individual's survival in some way after physical death. Such evidence is often housed in elaborate tombs with gifts from the material world that most likely were intended to help the soul navigate the labyrinthine passage to the afterlife.

The soul is a cornerstone of folklore. Its connection to the individual, its origin and eternal nature, its association with a higher power—all these things have been debated for millennia with varying conclusions. The evolutionary structure of worldwide folkloric drift, which in many ways resembles the glacial development of language, predictably produced a panoply of speculative suppositions about this provocative subject. Over time, the world's great wisdom traditions, which we usually label as "religions," have affirmed the reality of an eternal essence and expanded on the concept to help answer our most searching questions about what we are and what our purpose might be on this watery little planet.

Most of us have questions about what a soul is, how it operates and even if there is something we might call a "collective soul" that joins us all together in some way. While the world's wisdom traditions teach that human beings possess a soul or a spirit, those fundamental questions are seldom addressed in any meaningful detail. More recent wisdom traditions teach that the soul survives the physical death of the individual to exist in an eternal "afterlife," which might be quite pleasant for those who have adhered sufficiently to the tenants of a particular tradition but might be exceedingly unpleasant for those judged to have fallen short. Eternal damnation or reincarnation to a lower form of existence are examples of what can happen to recalcitrant souls according to some religious schools of thought.

This is a big topic in which metaphorical Scriptures can be misunderstood as literal, and thousands of different religious doctrines compete for the mind space of truth-seekers. To begin this journey of discovery we must first examine the station of human beings in the world of creation and the concept of the human soul.

Our material world can be categorized into five distinct realms of existence—mineral, plant, animal, human and divine.[10] Our most recent wisdom tradition explains that each realm has its own distinguishing qualities. Beginning with the mineral realm, each succeeding level builds upon the qualities of the realms below it and becomes more complex in its organization. While these realms of existence are distinct from each other, they are nevertheless interrelated.

The simplest level is the realm of minerals. Existence is its only quality. Consider, for example, a piece of granite or a diamond. It cannot grow, reproduce or move. It simply exists, yet it has a more complex and organized pattern of elements than non-existence.

The second level, the realm of plants, builds upon the simple quality of existence through its capacity to grow and reproduce. A small seed can grow and eventually bear fruit according to the genetic

---

10   'Abdu'l-Bahá, *The Promulgation of Universal Peace.*

information contained within its cellular structure. The plant and the elements from which it is made exist in a more complex organized form than a rock.

The third level is the realm of the animal. More complex and organized than the inhabitants of the lower realms, animals possess the qualities of sensory perception—sight, hearing, touch and taste— as well as the ability to move, grow and reproduce. Animal behavior is highly dependent upon the senses and instinct. Each animal contains genetic information that may dictate paths of migration, patterns of reproduction and other unique behaviors. Constant movement is often essential for survival, and so animals may constantly search for food and water as well as a safe place to reproduce and care for their offspring. In many cases, animals have shown the ability to understand and respond appropriately to spoken words.

The fourth level is the realm of humans, who possess all the qualities of the lower realms—existence, growth, reproduction, sensory perception and movement—but have unique qualities that distinguish them from the animal realm.

Unique Qualities of the Human Realm

Interestingly, though, many animals far exceed humans in their ability to see, feel, smell, hear, taste and move independently. These abilities, then, cannot distinguish humans from animals. No, the main distinguishing quality of humans is the ability to think, reason, use their imaginations and make moral decisions. Only humans have language because only humans are capable of rule-based abstract signing. Animals can often employ complex signals like gestures and sounds, but no animal uses rule-based designators. Animals live—and think—through their senses. Temple Grandin, the noted author on autism and professor of animal science, wrote, "Without verbal language, [animals] store memories of previous experiences as pictures, sounds, smells, tastes, or touch memories. Sensory-based thinking and memories are recollections of experiences without words."[11] With the enhanced capacity of an expanded language, humans have a profoundly elevated ability to think and reason.

> The reality of man is his thought, not his material body. The thought force and the animal force are partners. Although man is part of the animal creation, he possesses a power of thought superior to all other created beings. If a man's thought is constantly aspiring towards heavenly subjects, then does he become saintly; if on the other hand his thought does not soar, but is directed downwards to center itself upon the things of this world, he grows more and more material until he arrives at a state little better than that of a mere animal.[12]

Each realm of creation is unique and operates within its own level of development. But it may appear that there are exceptions to this general rule and that lower levels of existence may occasionally have some of the qualities of higher levels. For example, in the mineral realm some stones like calcium stalactites in caves can grow as more calcium is deposited on their surfaces. However, this is not the kind of growth from within that typifies the plant realm.

Similarly, some plants may move in response to the sun, but this level of movement cannot compare with the movement required in the animal realm. Animals have a limited ability to communicate, learn new behaviors or show a degree of attachment and sacrifice for other animals and humans. However, these signs of animal intelligence cannot compare with humans.

Consider a seed. Insignificant as it may be, it contains all the potentialities of a mighty tree, which it may become if the environmental conditions are suitable, and the seed is protected from

---

11   Temple Grandin, *Visual Thinking: The Hidden Gifts of People Who Think in Pictures, Patterns, and Abstractions.*

12   'Abdu'l-Bahá, *Paris Talks*, pp. 17–18.

outside damage. Human beings do not have the potential to become divine—which is the final realm of existence—but like a seed, they have the capacity to develop into a person with divine attributes.

From the moment of conception, every human being has the capacity for rational thought, which distinguishes them from the animal realm. As the fetus develops and a child is born and matures, the child's latent intelligence manifests.

Humans have the potential for great good. Unlike the animal realm, human actions are not bound by instinct alone. Human potential is determined by an individual's free will—the choice to use intelligence for good or otherwise. It is the human's rational soul, our higher human nature, that motivates us to rise above the physical demands of the material world and seek to improve our individual and collective life.

> The human spirit which distinguishes man from the animal is the rational soul; and these two names—the human spirit and the rational soul—designate one thing. This spirit, which in the terminology of the philosophers is the rational soul, encompasses all things and, as far as human capacity permits, discovers their realities and becomes aware of the properties and effects, the characteristics and conditions of earthly things.[13]

Rational thinking, of course, is an operation of the human mind, and so the mind must be related in some way to the "rational soul" referred to in the passage above. Because these concepts are abstract, the following metaphors can aid us in understanding this relationship:

> As for the mind, it is the power of the human spirit. The spirit is as the lamp, and the mind as the light that shines from it. The spirit is as the tree, and the mind as

---

13 'Abdu'l-Bahá, *Some Answered Questions*, pp. 208–209.

> the fruit. The mind is the perfection of the spirit and a necessary attribute thereof, even as the rays of the sun are an essential requirement of the sun itself.[14]

> That which is found to be real and conformable to reason must be accepted, and whatever science and reason cannot support must be rejected as imitation and not reality. Then differences of belief will disappear. All will become as one family, one people, and the same susceptibility to the divine bounty and education will be witnessed among mankind...[15]

The human spirit is mentioned in all the Scriptures of the world's wisdom traditions. The immortality or everlasting life of the spirit is a fundamental belief taught by all the Divine Educators. Because the spirit is not of the material world, it is not bound by time. The human spirit is sometimes referred to as our rational soul. It is the rational soul that separates us from the animal kingdom and makes us the highest level of creation on our planet.

Closely related to the rational soul is the powerful, unexplainable entity called the "mind," which science has always struggled to adequately define. For a time, scientists tried to define the mind as the product of brain activity. The brain was seen as the physical substance in this equation, and the mind was a conscious product of neurons firing. The brain undoubtedly plays an important role, but the mind cannot be confined to what is inside our head, or even our body. This concept has since been supported by research across the sciences.[16]

The connection of the mind to the rational soul is identified by 'Abdu'l-Bahá, the expounder of many theses and dialogues from a wisdom tradition called The Bahá'í Faith.

---

14   'Abdu'l-Bahá, *Bahá'í World Faith* - Abdu'l-Baha Section, p. 316

15   'Abdu'l-Bahá, *The Promulgation of Universal Peace*, p. 176.

16   https://qz.com/866352/scientists-say-your-mind-isn't-confined-to-your-brain-or-even-your-body.

Sometimes a physical disability may seem to diminish the strengths of an individual, but such disabilities cannot affect a person's soul. In fact, when the body is affected by a physical disability, the light of that person's intelligence may radiate even stronger. Consider, for example, the genius of the German musician Ludwig van Beethoven (1770-1827), who composed musical masterpieces despite the loss of his hearing; or Helen Keller (1880-1968), an American who lost both hearing and sight at an early age but went on to complete university and become an eloquent inspirational speaker. More recently, the wide-ranging knowledge of the English scientist Stephen Hawking (1942-2018) continued to inspire the world despite his fifty-year battle with a slowly progressing motor-neuron disease (ALS) that left him totally paralyzed and only able to communicate with the use of speech-generating devices.

The human soul, then, is closely linked to rational thinking, which lifts us up to our higher human nature and brings us joy and despair. To paraphrase René Descartes: "We think therefore we are."

Each of the four realms described above is distinguished by a higher level of organization than the preceding one. The plant realm, for example, is more organized than the mineral realm. The proof of this is that upon death, plants, animals and humans return to the least organized form—the mineral realm.

Rational Proofs for the Existence of the Soul

Throughout history, the concept of the human soul has been based on belief. Since the human soul is not a material thing—it cannot be seen or touched or physically measured—it may not seem possible to define it in a scientific manner. It can be explained, however, in a rational manner through reasoning and logical deduction.

Consider this truth: Whatever is created cannot explain its creator because the creation is at a level below its creator. For example, a wooden chair cannot comprehend or explain the carpenter who created it. Yet we know that the carpenter exists because of the chair, which required someone to make it. The beauty or more highly organized form of the chair provides evidence of the qualities of the carpenter, but the chair itself cannot adequately describe its creator.

Similarly, many concepts in the human realm cannot be defined in a physical manner but can be easily understood through rational thinking because their existence is evident from their effects. Consider all types of emotions. Even though emotions such as love, hate, attraction, joy and sadness are not physically measurable, their effects on our bodies can be measured, and the otherwise unseen emotions can alter our view of the world and influence how we live our lives.

The concept of black holes gives us a good example of how such deductive reasoning works. A black hole is a region of spacetime where gravity is so strong that nothing, not even light has enough energy to escape. A black hole cannot be seen, but its effects on the behavior of the universe can be measured, which provides proof that the black hole exists. Thus, rational thinking has proven with solid evidence that black holes not only exist, but that there are approximately 40 billion billion of them in the universe (40 followed by eighteen zeros.)[17]

Creation and the Evolution of Life

In this book, we use the noun "creation" to mean a new existence. There are two possible paths for any new creation—to come from another form of existence while possessing a greater organization, or to come from pure nonexistence. We use the term "evolution" to mean the creation of something that progresses from something else. This is different than simple change such as occurs when an organism grows from a seed to a tree or from a fertilized egg into an infant and eventually into an adult before dying.

---

17   https://www.iflscience.com/there-are-an-estimated-40-billion-billion-black-holes-in-the-universe-62296.

The First Law of Thermodynamics

All scientific systems like physics, chemistry and medicine are based on the principle that energy cannot be created or destroyed. Energy can only be transformed or changed into matter, something that can be seen and touched. Energy and matter, therefore, are really just different forms of the same thing. This scientific law, called the First Law of Thermodynamics, is the cornerstone of all scientific advancement.

The Second Law of Thermodynamics

The Second Law of Thermodynamics defines the concept of entropy, stating that the physical world tends to move toward disorder or decomposition unless there is an infusion of energy from an outside force to maintain its organized form. Any change from a more organized form to a less organized one means that less energy is required to maintain its lesser organized form. This process of energy preservation is called disintegration.

For example, the carpenter, after *thinking through* the creation of a table from a piece of wood, can then apply his energy to the physical act of creating the table, which transforms the raw wood into a more organized form. The carpenter has reshaped the wood to create a table. In another example, a child who is playing with blocks can apply thinking and energy to build a pyramid, a more highly organized arrangement of the blocks. Creation, therefore, is relative to the state of organization.

In nature, when a tree has access to all the elements needed for growth it will flourish. If one of the elements goes missing, the tree dies and decomposes into the basic elements of carbon, hydrogen, oxygen and nitrogen.

The opposite of decomposition is composition and evolution, which can be easily seen within the plant, animal and human realms. A seed does not look like the tree that it will become, yet within its DNA lies the potential to become a tree.

...let us suppose that man once walked on all fours or had a tail: This change and transformation is similar to that of the fetus in the womb of the mother. Even though the fetus develops and evolves in every possible way before it reaches its full development, from the beginning it belongs to a distinct species. The same holds true in the vegetable kingdom, where we observe that the original and distinctive character of the species does not change, while its form, colour, and mass do change, transform, and evolve.[18]

To summarize: Just as man progresses, evolves, and is transformed from one form and appearance to another in the womb of the mother, while remaining from the beginning a human embryo, so too has man remained a distinct essence—that is, the human species—from the beginning of his formation in the matrix of the world, and has passed gradually from form to form. It follows that this change of appearance, this evolution of organs, and this growth and development do not preclude the originality of the species. Now, even accepting the reality of evolution and progress, nevertheless, from the moment of his appearance man has possessed perfect composition, and has had the capacity and potential to acquire both material and spiritual perfections and to become the embodiment of the verse, "Let Us make man in Our image, after Our likeness." At most, he has become more pleasing, more refined and graceful, and by virtue of civilization he has emerged from his wild state, just as the wild fruits become finer and sweeter under the cultivation of the gardener, and acquire ever greater delicacy and vitality.[19]

---

18 'Abdu'l-Bahá, *Some Answeered Questions.*
19 'Abdu'l-Bahá, *Some Answered Questions*, chapter 49.

The seed does not move from one realm of existence to another. It continues to exist in the plant realm. So, the question arises… can the concept of evolution be applied to each of the four lower realms of existence—mineral, plant, animal and human—or is an outside power required to infuse a new impulse into each of these realms to allow advancement from one realm to another? Rationally, the advancement between the realms of creation in this world—say, from the animal realm to the human realm—requires an infusion of energy from an external source, such as a higher power. Even though this power is beyond our ability to fully understand or define, an external, non-material force explains the creation of such a more organized existence. Scientific principles and laws provide evidence that supports the existence of such an entity, which in some cases is called the realm of Divinity or "Spirit."

Creation Stories

Around the world, traditional cultures each have their own creation story. Many of these stories have not been written down until recently. Other stories have been recorded as part of the Holy Scriptures and are better known. The story of the creation of the world is the first topic in the Old Testament, the Holy Scriptures of the Jewish Faith, and is accepted by Christians and Muslims alike. Similar stories of creation can be seen in other cultures and traditions pre-dating the version in the Bible. These myths evolved over time and eventually became hardened into loyalty-based beliefs. Such origin stories carry wisdom if not historical truth. What can humans in the twenty-first century glean from these creation stories?

According to the book of Genesis, God created the world in six days, and on the seventh day He rested. Day by day, He brought into being different parts of the world. On the third day, He created the sun. Genesis uses the word "day" but does not define that term. Does "day" mean the time it takes for Earth to make one revolution on its axis as it rotates around the sun, which takes about twenty-four hours? Or does "day" imply a longer period because so much was created on each of the six days? Some believe we should not question this because God is able to do as much as He wants in the twinkling of an eye. But that belief is not reasonable because we know from scientific investigation and evidence that God did not create the world in six days. Rather than blind faith, rational thinking helps us arrive at the proper conclusion. Is it not possible to understand the evolutionary nature of folklore and then analyze each part of the creation story as a symbol for some deeper meaning rather than just the literal description of physical reality?

A rational explanation of the creation story in Genesis might alternatively suggest that creation was a continuous process over a long period of time. Metaphorically, it may be suggesting that as man gradually became aware of certain realities in this world—the concept of time in relation to the sun and the moon; the existence of the diversity of plants and animals with all of their wonders; hidden meanings discovered in God's "creation"— it seemed as if the world was being created before his eyes, though it had existed before man's awareness of it. The seven days of creation may also refer to the various stages of humanity's coming of age.

What is your takeaway from this story? Perhaps the story of Adam and Eve represents the gradual maturation of rational thinking, the development of judgement and moral choices and the building of relationships between people. In this way, the concepts of creation and evolution could both be true, though in different contexts.

There is little doubt that humans have evolved physically over millennia and in different geographies and climates. But, to many people, there is also little doubt that this entity we call the human spirit or rational soul must have had a Creator with a higher intelligence. A chair cannot create another chair. It takes a skilled carpenter from a higher realm to make a chair. Likewise, it seems unlikely that a human evolved from a lower existence, but rather through the intervention of a higher realm, one which many call the Divine.

The Purpose of Our Creation

The universal question that we all have, of course, is that if we were created—why? For what purpose? Why are we here? A mystical poem of ancient Persia describes the true purpose of human life as our effort to reach the Divine.

> Thou, I testify, the human temple is honorably refined,
> Yet the garment's beauty of humanity is no sign.
> For mankind will soar until it sees naught but the Divine.
> Observe then how noble its attire, its heights how sublime.[20]

The Divine is unknowable to us because we are of a lower realm. The created cannot fully comprehend the nature of the Creator in the divine realm. The only way that we can strive to "reach the Divine" and gain a very limited understanding of the nature of God is by turning to the revelations that have been given to us by His chosen Messengers. The Holy Scriptures are a record of these revelations or guidance from God as well as the history of the life of many of these Messengers, who are also called Manifestations of the Divine.

The spiritual guidance provided by the Scriptures of all the great wisdom traditions is consistent. To summarize what we have been told, the purpose of this life is to know and worship the Divine and to strive to follow the principles revealed by the Divine for our spiritual development. The following words revealed by the latest Divine Educator beautifully express God's purpose in creating this world and all humanity:

> O Son of Man! Veiled in My immemorial being and in the ancient eternity of My essence, I knew My love for thee; therefore I created thee, have engraved on thee Mine image and revealed to thee My beauty.[21]

---

20 Poem by Saadi (approximately 1210-1291 AD), famous Persian poet; translation by Linda Kazemzadeh.

21 Bahá'u'lláh *The Hidden Words of Bahá'u'lláh.*

> O Son of Man! I loved thy creation, hence I created thee. Wherefore, do thou love Me, that I may name thy name and fill thy soul with the spirit of life.[22]

In addition, Scriptures urge us to develop spiritually by acquiring virtues or divine qualities that can help us collectively establish the unity of humankind. As expressed in the Old Testament, our purpose is to become like the image of God[23]—in other words, to mirror Him in our lives by reflecting His unity. The "image of God" has nothing to do with visual likeness, which would be impossible since God is not human and has no material existence. The purpose of every Divine Educator is to give us the guidance and encouragement to accomplish this.

Truthfulness is one of the cornerstone virtues that we are called upon to acquire.

> Truthfulness is the foundation of all human virtues. Without truthfulness progress and success, in all the worlds of God, are impossible for any soul. When this holy attribute is established in man, all the divine qualities will also be acquired.[24]

To better understand spiritual development, consider the physical development of a child in the womb. Over the course of nine months, the child develops the physical features it needs for a healthy life in this world. If it does not properly develop sight or hearing, or arms or legs, we say that the infant is born with physical handicaps. Similarly, our purpose in this world, like that fetus, is to develop the

---

22 Bahá'u'lláh, *The Hidden Words of Bahá'u'lláh*, from the Arabic, Numbers 3-4.

23 *Bible*, Genesis 1: 27, "So God created man in his *own* image, in the image of God created he him; male and female created he them."

24 'Abdu'l-Bahá, quoted in Shoghi Effendi, *The Advent of Divine Justice*, p. 22.

divine virtues—the spiritual senses and attributes—that prepare us to enter the world to come without any spiritual handicaps.

During our physical life, we are called upon to help advance the goals of humanity for the time in which we live. Doing so has two significant benefits. It helps us achieve a more peaceful and just society for everyone and nourishes our personal spiritual development.

At this point in history, humanity's most important goal is to recognize and promote the oneness of humankind. All other goals orbit around the sun of this central principle. Every individual can contribute to the universal acceptance of this truth. To achieve this requires us all to eliminate our prejudices—racial, religious, political, national, cultural and social. Eliminating our prejudices would uproot the cause of so much disunity and social injustice.

What if all of us considered our work—whatever it is, paid or unpaid—to be a personal and unselfish service to humanity and a way to worship our Creator through that service? Just about any kind of productive work or career choice can benefit humanity directly or indirectly. Maybe our work and our attitudes about it would improve, and we would acquire important virtues at the same time. If you believe in the main tenets of the Bible, this is perhaps what bringing about the Kingdom of God on Earth really means.

The Unknowable Divine Realm

The divine realm has the power to: join atoms into molecules to form the mineral realm; guide growth and reproduction in the plant realm; organize and stimulate growth, reproduction and movement in the animal realm; and in the human realm, to foster intelligence and imagination (the rational soul).

Throughout recorded history, humans have striven to understand creation, calling it by different names according to their own perceptions and beliefs. Some hold beliefs in another realm that exists beyond the human realm, one that affects all the realms of creation in this world. We call this the divine realm, and it is a lovely, comforting concept consistent with humanity's extraordinary ability to find ways to survive.

You may conclude that the soul is merely a human construct, an escape mechanism from death. But, what if it isn't that? What if the soul is an integral part of life and, like energy, is indestructible? What a wonderful journey we are missing by dividing ourselves into small sects with only partial understanding, and many misunderstandings, about our spiritual nature and then killing one another over territory and insignificant details espoused by ill-informed ministers of faith. Living as if each of us possesses an eternal soul may be the healthiest expression of our shared humanity. In this book, we try to show that love for each other's souls is a way to unify all mankind.

The following names and many others are an attempt by diverse believers to describe this divine realm in human terms:

- Creator
- The Unknowable Essence
- The Source of All Being
- Ahura Mazda
- God
- Brahman
- Jehovah
- Alláh

This divine realm of the unknown is open to all humans and can be used to extract new ideas and unknown concepts that can drive arts and science forward. The world of divinity can neither be entered or exited, nor can it be touched or seen. It has no beginning and no end. It exists without attachment or relevance to this world and is independent from any limitation.

While the term "the Kingdom of God" is often used as a reference to "heaven," that term may be merely an expression of what it is like, not a reality, because heaven is certainly not a physical location. It is sanctified above time and place—a spiritual realm, a divine world, and for some a comforting metaphor. For the divine realm to exist, it must be exalted above physical bodies and freed from the idle conjectures of men. For to be confined to a place is a characteristic of bodies, not of spirits. Time and place encompass the body, not the soul.

> From experience we know that the body of man abides in a limited space and occupies no more than two spans of earth. But the spirit and mind of man traverses all countries and regions and even the limitless expanse of the heavens; it encompasses all existence and makes discoveries in the spheres above and in the infinite reaches of the universe. This is because the spirit has no place: It is a placeless reality, and for the spirit earth and heaven are the same, since it makes discoveries in both. But the body is confined in space and is unaware of that which lies beyond.[25]

---

25 'Abdu'l-Bahá, *Some Answered Questions*, p. 280

Chapter 3:
The Soul

Rational thinking, which means "thinking with reason," refers to an ability to draw sensible conclusions from facts, logic and data. In other words, if your thoughts are based on facts and not emotions, you are engaged in rational thinking.

Scientists use three types of investigations to research and develop explanations for events in nature: descriptive investigation, comparative investigation, and experimental investigation. When dealing with non-material topics, we can still be scientific by using descriptive and comparative investigation techniques and then applying rational thinking to reach the correct conclusion.

Regarding the soul, most people agree it exists, but some consider the concept to be irrational. Obviously, this topic needs deeper investigation. Classically, the "soul" has been thought of as the immaterial essence of a human being and the spiritual principle embodied in all rational and spiritual beings. Most wisdom traditions that speak of the soul consider it to be immortal. In referring to the soul, the authors prefer to use the more descriptive term "rational soul," which is discussed below.

The Rational Soul

Putting the words "rational" and "soul" together suggests that the soul has an independent existence apart from the body—the animating principle of human life as distinguished from animal or vegetable life. For Plato, this rational soul is the thinking element in every human being that decides what is factual and merely obvious, judges what is factual and what is untrue, and intelligently makes sensible decisions.[26]

The term "rational soul" was first used by the Greek philosopher Aristotle to mean "the actuality of a body that has life" and "the part responsible for reason." The Bahá'í Faith provides greater clarity:

> Now regarding the question whether the faculties of the mind and the human soul are one and the same. These faculties are but the inherent properties of the soul, such as the power of imagination, of thought, of understanding; powers that are the essential requisites of the reality of man, even as the solar ray is the inherent property of the sun. The temple of man is like unto a mirror, his soul is as the sun, and his mental faculties even as the rays that emanate from that source of light. The ray may cease to fall upon the mirror, but it can in no wise be dissociated from the sun.[27]

Thus, the term "rational soul" alludes to the soul as being inherently "rational" even though it is not rationality itself. Rationality, or the rational mind, is but one of the faculties of the soul.

When the world's wisdom traditions present the concept of a soul, the references are vague, which allows those with imaginations to fill in the blanks. Of all the wisdom traditions, the Bahá'í Faith presents the deepest explanation of the soul, which is often called the "rational soul." But when studying the Bahá'í Writings about the body,

---

26 Plato, *Plato's Republic Book IV*.
27 'Abdu'l-Bahá, *Tablet to August Forel*.

soul and spirit in English, we are still handicapped by a lack of clarity because the Writings were not all translated by the same person, and some terms lack a perfect English corollary. In some cases, the words "soul" and "spirit" were used interchangeably because of translation difficulties. Nevertheless, these Writings definitively express that...

> ...we have three aspects of our humanness, so to speak, a body, a mind and an immortal identity—soul or spirit. ... the mind forms a link between the soul and the body, and the two interact on each other.[28]

According to this passage, the mind is a kind of intermediary between the body and soul. The Writings also confirm the immortality of the soul:

> All the differing degrees of created physical beings are limited, but the soul is limitless! In all religions the belief exists that the soul survives the death of the body.[29]

Science still has not adequately defined the mind of a human being, though no one doubts that it exists. The mind is closely interrelated to the body and the soul, but...

> ...in the world of dreams the soul sees when the eyes are closed. The man is seemingly dead, lies there as dead; the ears do not hear, yet he hears. The body lies there, but he—that is, the soul—travels, sees, observes. All the instruments of the body are inactive, all the functions seemingly useless. Notwithstanding this, there is an immediate and vivid perception by the soul. Exhilaration is experienced. The soul journeys, perceives, senses. It often happens that a man in a

---

28   Shoghi Effendi, quoted in Arohanui, *Letters from Shoghi Effendi to New Zealand*, p. 89.

29   'Abdu'l-Bahá, *Paris Talks*, pp. 89–90.

> state of wakefulness has not been able to accomplish the solution of a problem, and when he goes to sleep, he will reach that solution in a dream. How often it has happened that he has dreamed, even as the prophets have dreamed, of the future; and events which have thus been foreshadowed have come to pass literally.[30]

But the soul is neither inside the body nor outside as it is not of this world. Thus, it can neither enter nor exit the body. It shines forth in the contingent world only when it associates with the body. The details of how these intertwined entities work together are largely unknown; perhaps the mind's relationship to the soul is what provides a rational faculty to the soul.

> As outer circumstances are communicated to the soul by the eyes, ears, and brain of a man, so does the soul communicate its desires and purposes through the brain to the hands and tongue of the physical body, thereby expressing itself.[31]

The superiority of the soul over the body is emphasized in these words...

> ...is not the light superior ... to the lamp which holds it? However beautiful the form of the lamp may be, if the light is not there its purpose is unfulfilled, it is without life—a dead thing. The lamp needs the light, but the light does not need the lamp. [Likewise] The spirit [soul] does not need a body, but the body needs spirit, or it cannot live. The soul can live without a body, but the body without a soul dies.[32]

---

30 'Abdu'l-Bahá, *The Promulgation of Universal Peace*, p. 416.

31 'Abdu'l-Bahá, *Paris Talks*, p. 86.

32 'Abdu'l-Bahá, *Paris Talks*, pp. 86–87.

Rational Thinking Does Not Prevent Error

After referring to the ancient philosophers as "pillars of wisdom," 'Abdu'l-Baha used them to warn that even rational thinking, while necessary to test arguments and discern truth, is subject to error.

> **They proved things by reason and hold firmly to logical proofs; all their arguments are arguments of reason. Notwithstanding this, they differed greatly, and their opinions were contradictory. They even changed their views... Plato at first logically proved the immobility of the earth and the movement of the sun; later by logical arguments he proved that the sun was the stationary center, and that the earth was moving... Therefore, it is evident that the method of reason is not perfect, for the differences of the ancient philosophers, the want of stability and the variations of their opinions, prove this. For if it were perfect, all ought to be united in their ideas and agreed in their opinions.[33]**

With this type of reason, buttressed by caution, we have decided to reevaluate the Scriptures of the past to find solutions for today's problems.

> **Every subject presented to a thoughtful audience must be supported by rational proofs and logical arguments. Proofs are of four kinds: first, through sense perception; second, through the reasoning faculty; third, from traditional or scriptural authority; fourth, through the medium of inspiration.[34]**

All four kinds of proof are subject to error, but fortunately "the grace of the Holy Spirit is the true criterion" for gaining certitude.[35]

---

33 *A Compilation on Scholarship*, p. 23; Available at: https://www.bahai.org/library/authoritative-texts/compilations/scholarship/.

34 'Abdu'l-Bahá, *The Promulgation of Universal Peace*, p. 253

35 'Abdu'l-Bahá, *Some Answered Questions*, chapter 83.

Even in choosing the truth from a Divine Educator, it is written that we must use rational thinking to make sure we are not establishing our faith on a false basis.

> If thou wishest the divine knowledge and recognition, purify thy heart from all beside God, be wholly attracted to the ideal, beloved One; search for and choose Him and apply thyself to rational and authoritative arguments. For arguments are a guide to the path and by this the heart will be turned unto the Sun of Truth.[36]

> The yearning for belief is inextinguishable, an inherent part of what makes one human. When it is blocked or betrayed, the rational soul is driven to seek some new compass point, however inadequate or unworthy, around which it can organize experience and dare again to assume the risks that are an inescapable aspect of life.[37]

As humans, we seek logical explanations before fully accepting an idea. If our acceptance is gained by illogical and faith-based emotional proofs, then our allegiance to the idea can erode over time and be replaced by a more rational idea. This may explain today's large exodus from religious institutions.

> Every religion which is not in accordance with established science is superstition. Religion must be reasonable. If it does not square with reason, it is superstition and without foundation. It is like a mirage, which deceives man by leading him to think it is a body of water. God has endowed man with reason that he may perceive what is true. If we insist that such and such a

---

36 'Abdu'l-Bahá, *Tablets of 'Abdu'l-Bahá Abbas, vol. 1*, p. 384
37 *Century of Light*, commissioned by the Universal House of Justice, p. 60

> subject is not to be reasoned out and tested according to the established logical modes of the intellect, what is the use of the reason which God has given man?[38]

The Soul of Humanity

Humanity is a term that refers collectively to all humans who live on this planet. Since the authors believe that individuals possess a soul, it is fair, then, to question if the collective life of humanity also has a soul—or, in other words, a collective mindset.

To answer this provocative question, we must first understand that the nature of the collection of humans we call humanity mirrors the nature of an individual in two fundamental ways. The human soul and the soul of humanity both possess a material or "lower" nature shared with the animal realm. This nature focuses on survival and receives its information about the world from the five senses.

But the human soul and the soul of humanity also have a non-material or "higher" human nature distinguished by human intelligence—the "rational soul." While the lower nature fights for the individual's existence at all costs— the animal instinct of "survival of the fittest"—the higher nature strives to protect the survival of humanity, which depends on the unity of its members. The lower nature, often called childish, is selfish and self-absorbed. By contrast, the higher nature, often referred to as wise, is selfless and willing to make sacrifices to ensure the peace and well-being of humanity.

> The first condition of perception in the world of nature is the perception of the rational soul. In this perception and in this power all men are sharers, whether they be neglectful or vigilant, believers or deniers... The power of the rational soul can discover the realities of things, comprehend the peculiarities of beings, and penetrate the mysteries of existence. All sciences, knowledge,

---

38 'Abdu'l-Bahá, *The Promulgation of Universal Peace*, Pages 64

> arts, wonders, institutions, discoveries and enterprises come from the exercised intelligence of the rational soul.[39]

The collective mindset the authors call the soul of humanity has the capacity to reason and make choices for the benefit of all humanity. Unfortunately, many barriers—chief among them disunity and adherence to outdated beliefs and traditions—often prevent good decisions and undermine positive results. We refer to the unique customs of a group that are generally shaped by religious and other beliefs as a "culture." The existence worldwide of so many different cultures is proof of a great diversity in beliefs. More importantly, however, these numerous cultures have become a major barrier for the unification of humankind.

Humans have inhabited Earth for a long time. To determine if the soul of humanity is advancing or not, we can ask simple questions. Are people today still bound by the harmful aspects and prejudices of their traditional cultures? Is the soul of humanity more multi-cultural or world-embracing than it was a hundred years ago? Are there any signs of the development of a global culture that may unify mankind?

A quick survey of world history is not encouraging. Cultural differences have led people to find ways to segregate themselves from those with a different culture. Over time, people divided themselves over imaginary national borders, belief systems and religions, skin color, et cetera. These developments were not rational but were mostly based on blind faith in untested "truths," a desire to differentiate one group as superior over another or motives of gaining profit or power. Emotional forces frequently warp rational deduction. They allow beliefs to be based on ignorance or cause an individual to cling to a cherished belief that in fact blinds the individual and his or her community to that concept's irrationality.

---

39 'Abdu'l-Bahá, *Some Answered Questions*, pp. 217-218

Uncovering Truth

Every civilization has struggled with its course-setting task of defining the purpose of life. Ancient philosophers such as Socrates, Plato and Aristotle spent most of their lives debating and writing about this topic as it relates to ethics, politics and justice. In more recent times, many philosophers and visionaries have continued the search for meaning.[40]

The basic topic of what is truth has dominated discussion among deep thinkers in religious, political, social and scientific fields. Recently, political and religious debates have become heated over whether there are such things as alternative facts and truths.

Human intelligence governed by rational thinking is how we assess new information and determine whether it is true or false. In the broadest sense, the fundamental purpose is to determine whether the information will benefit or harm individuals and humanity. Assessing truth requires careful consideration of relevant facts such as the following:

- Is our assessment based on scientific data or simply agreement with the conclusions of someone we trust or admire?
- How can we determine what is true information backed by authenticated data from reputable sources or what is merely hearsay?
- How can we have reasonable discussions and make rational decisions if we cannot agree on the sources of our information?

---

40 See René Descartes (1596-1650, French mathematician and scientist), Immanuel Kant (1724-1804, German philosopher), Friedrich Nietzsche (1844-1900, German philosopher), Max Ludwig Planck (1858-1947, German physicist, Nobel Prize winner, 1918) and Francis Collins (1950-present, American physician, geneticist leading Human Genome Project). Of particular note are Nietzsche's publications *Beyond Good and Evil* (1886), *A Genealogy of Morals* (1887) and *Thus Spake Zarathustra* (1883-92). Moreover, refer to writings of Bahá'u'lláh (1819-1892) and 'Abdu'l-Bahá (1844-1921), particularly *Some Answered Questions*.

- Is our assessment of truth based on wishful thinking or personal bias?
- Has our own intellectual vanity clouded our assessment of the truth?
- What role do our feelings play in differentiating between truth and falsehood?

Traditionally, cultures have had their own proprietary sources of trusted information, thought patterns, totems and values, all of which contributed to a unique belief system about the universe and how it operates. If something could not be explained or understood, it was often attributed to a supernatural or superhuman force. When understanding is not based on verified facts about reality, however, the result is ignorance and superstition. Ignorance, whether in the past or the present, can become so entrenched in a culture that the crooked seems straight and half-truths can mislead the population, resulting in disunity and division. Systemic ignorance and superstition has led to disastrous fanaticism and prejudices with no rational basis.

One insightful definition of prejudice is "an emotional commitment to ignorance."[41] Unfortunately, fanaticism and prejudice are common in cultures at every stage of material development. The result is chaos, confusion, disunity, discord and even war. Clearly, it is possible to use half-truths and invented information to persuade great swaths of humanity to reach erroneous conclusions.

Today, political and thought leaders exert a great influence on humanity. Each exhorts followers to accept his or her own "truths," which may be based on a made-up story or personal belief in the integrity and accuracy of their sources. The tunnel vision of absolute belief prevents these leaders from detecting when data sources are corrupt, or the information is unverified. Fervent followers can be

---

41   Rutstein, Nathan. *Healing Racism in America*, Whitcomb Publishing 1993, p. 42.

easily deceived, misguided and even hijacked into violence to protect their unfounded beliefs.

Examples of such deception can be seen in advertising that persuades the public to buy a certain product or switch loyalty from one brand to another. Information in ads may be true, partly true or false. Without fact-checking, the consumer yields great power to sponsors, leaders of thought and political systems. When political ads are used to boost the popularity and power of a candidate, a rational person would question whether the information is true and either beneficial or harmful to individuals and humanity. But most of us get swept into the slipstream of persuasive half-truths and lies.

Even news and information from mainstream and trusted sources cannot be totally accepted anymore. The line has been blurred between objective news reporting, opinions and "analysis," and "infotainment" such as biased documentaries. Too often, believing they are being presented facts, audiences let unchallenged misinformation influence their conclusions and actions. It has taken a long time to reach this state of uncertainty about truth, and now this uncertainty has bled into distrust of science by segments of society. Consider the ferocious anti-vaccine movement during the Covid pandemic. Misinformation is not always intentional, and when US public health officials made specific scientific declarations without adequate caveats, many people believed they were hearing proven facts rather than operating theories based on the best available information, which was predictably flawed. When more accurate information was learned and released, the appearance to the public was that science contained a lot of untruths.

Again, what is truth? Is it relative to an individual's perception or is there an absolute truth? Are new standards needed for universal truths that are acceptable to all of humanity? To answer these questions, consider that each individual and humanity are simultaneously advancing and expanding intellectually while living in a world of relative truth. Day by day, knowledge and understanding are increasing, which means that the "truth" we glean from the knowledge of today cannot be absolute for all time. It can only be absolute for a limited time until new knowledge provides new insights that may revise the "truth" that the older knowledge suggested. This means that truth can be both relative and absolute to its time.

Rational thinking, then, must be a continuous process of evaluation and reevaluation of knowledge as it develops over time. Are we up to this task? Can humans advance to a higher level of intellect and reasoning on their own? Is a creative power or energy from a higher realm—the divine realm—needed to spark the advancement of higher levels of collective thought and reasoning, which is the soul of humanity?

Establishing Unity of Thought

Unity and harmony are best promoted when a person's thinking is based on reason and understanding. Here is a simple example—the mathematical truth that $2 + 2 = 4$. All people with a basic knowledge of mathematical laws accept that equation as true, and all other numerical equations from algebra to calculus to differential equations depend on acceptance of this basic fact. This unity of thought promotes harmony and unity in dialogue since everyone agrees on that basic equation. It allows mathematicians, scientists, and physicists to communicate and learn from each other more easily and accurately.

When laws of mathematics and science are disregarded, however, ignorance and prejudice can overpower rational thoughts. When humanity deviates from scientific or rational thinking, even simple problems become insoluble. Reality becomes obscured. Disunity and division increase. Humanity can be misled and persuaded to make choices that are detrimental to its collective existence. In religion, false truths based on ignorance have frequently caused division even within a generally homogeneous sect. When verifiable data and scientific laws are uniformly applied to problems of the world, however, rational thinking promotes unity of thought.

In a sense, truth is but one point and ignorance divides it. It is like the old story of blind men touching different parts of an elephant and then trying to describe the whole animal. The man touching the tail believes the creature is long and skinny like a snake, but another, who touched only the foot, says it is a stumpy and large animal. All explanations contain some true elements but do not express the whole truth. If the blind men had consulted on their various experiences, they may have reached a conclusion closer to the greater truth.

Factors other than disagreement on facts can also sway the thinking of humanity. Consider these examples in which "love" means a preference for or attachment to something:

- love for a particular individual or family;
- love of one's racial or ethnic group;
- love of one's nation or political system;
- love of a particular idea or one's beliefs or faith.

Throughout time, the word "love" has acquired numerous shades of meaning, which can be confusing. Consider the different meanings in this simple sentence: "I love my shoes, I love my dog and I love you, my husband." This woman would probably give up her life for her husband, but would she readily give up her life for her shoes?

Generally, however, the word "love" refers to a passionate feeling, a non-logical attraction or commitment to one's country, one's ideas and faith, and (presumably with a bit less passion) for one's shoes and dog. A basic more rational definition of "love" is a sense or feeling of attraction.

A passionate commitment to something important can inspire an individual to greater acts of service and self-sacrifice, but when applied to the soul of humanity such emotional attachments can be irrational. They tend to compromise unity of thought and can lead to disunity within families, communities, nations and religions. Feelings and commitments can be valid sources of inspiration and motivation for individuals, but reason and verifiable facts are essential for the harmonious development of humanity.

Many people identify themselves with a political system, nation, race, religion, or even economic status within a society without knowing and accepting all aspects of the group with which they are associating. The unity of humanity requires rational thinking, even though the information available today is not an *absolute* truth and may change over time. The truth of today may not be the truth of tomorrow because our knowledge is exponentially increasing. However, rational thinking can be applied consistently to all aspects of our lives even as new facts and evidence emerge. In fact, rational thinking *requires* continuous updating of our beliefs to accommodate new knowledge. To disregard new information would be irrational.

Religious beliefs are very personal, of course. No two people feel the same way about religion, so it is difficult to bring unity between people based on religious feelings. But a degree of unity can be achieved when religion is considered as deeply personal and each person's feelings and beliefs about it are respected. Devotional activities can be practiced privately and not in groups that segregate some believers from others, yet meeting in groups can help transcend differences that can be disunifying. Rational discussions of various belief systems can have a unifying effect when done respectfully. The common point around which all people of faith can unite is a relationship with the Creator—which we intend to mean gaining more knowledge of the Creator's plan and purpose as revealed by the Divine Educators. The more this is based on rational thinking and not irrational belief, the more it can bring people together.

An early attempt to establish unity of thought in a large community was undertaken by the twelve tribes of Israel as documented in the Bible's Old Testament. The Ten Commandments revealed by Moses became a common foundation for advancing civilizations. Subsequently, Jesus Christ renewed the teachings of Moses and emphasized two foundational laws:

> Thou shalt love the Lord your God with all thy heart, and with all thy soul and with all thy mind. This is the first and great commandment. And the second is like unto it, Thou shalt love thy neighbor as thyself. On these two commandments hang all the law and the prophets.[42]

The unity of thought produced by the teachings of Jesus led to the establishment of the Christian civilization, which initially united Jews and Gentiles as neighbors from many different cultures.

Six hundred years later, Muhammad arose in Arabia, revealing teachings that united the war-torn tribes of Arabia into one nation that eventually embraced a multitude of ethnic groups in a vast Islamic Empire. In general, unity of thought promotes unity between people because they all have agreed on the basic reasoning.

Today, our greatest need is to unite humanity under common laws and principles based on rational thinking. In 1875, 'Abdu'l-Bahá commented in a treatise addressed to the people and rulers of Persia about the need to establish a "Union of the nations of the world."[43] In 1920, after the establishment of the League of Nations, he praised the institution as an important step toward the goal of unification but warned that the League was "incapable of establishing Universal Peace" because it failed to represent all nations and had insufficient power over member states.[44]

Later, this idea led to the establishment of the United Nations and the adoption of mutually acceptable standards and laws for humanity. Since its establishment in 1948, each resolution and statement has undergone rational consultation (though today influenced by national political and economic considerations) before a vote for adoption or rejection by the nations of the world. These

---

42 *Bible*, Mathew 22: 37-40.
43 'Abdu'l-Bahá, *The Secret of Divine Civilization*.
44 'Abdu'l-Bahá, *Selections from the Writings of 'Abdu'l-Bahá*.

agreements are gradually establishing a common understanding and unity of thought among many cultures, nationalities and religious communities.

Unfortunately, the United Nations, with its five-nation veto power, has become ineffectual. A new NATO (North Atlantic Treaty Organization) and other organizations are fortunately becoming more united and forceful against aggression by other countries in Europe. We are now seeing the seeds of new organizations in the Pacific and Middle East aimed at achieving greater unity and collective security for clusters of nations.

> The utterance of God is a lamp, whose light is these words: Ye are the fruits of one tree, and the leaves of one branch. Deal ye one with another with the utmost love and harmony, with friendliness and fellowship. So powerful is the light of unity that it can illuminate the whole earth.[45]

The concept of a Supreme Being, no matter how it is named or perceived, is a single point around which humanity can have a dialogue leading to the unification of humanity. An individual does not have to "believe in" or accept all the religious Scriptures that comprise the world's wisdom traditions, but evaluating them rationally can be a first step toward unity.

Proofs and Schools of Thought

Humanity has long struggled to establish proof for the existence of a higher entity that is the source of creation, particularly the source of the human soul and the energy needed to unite mankind.

Philosophical or Theological Proofs: Many philosophers and religions have attempted to prove the existence of a higher power by arguing that a creation needs a creator. Thus, the creation itself is evidence

---

45   Bahá'u'lláh, *Gleanings from the Writings of Bahá'u'lláh*, CXXXII, p. 288

that a creator exists. The qualities of the creation demonstrate the qualities of the creator. Most believers of the world's religions readily accept this concept. For those who are not believers of any religion, however, this proof is not very persuasive.

Teleological Proofs (Tele in Greek means "end" or "purpose" and -ology means "study of"): This proof focuses on the purpose of creation in the material world more than its cause. It suggests that explaining a spiritual concept with the limitations of human language is impossible, just as the created cannot explain the creator. The proof admits that the explanations of religious teachers cannot be proven or disproven since they rely on feelings and blind faith and not rational thinking.

Ontological Proofs (dealing with the nature and relations of being or existence): This proof is more general or global, putting the purpose of this unknowable world in perspective. It attempts to answer questions about humanity's purpose in the big scheme of things. For example, do we just live like animals and only focus on our own needs, or do we act responsibly for our planet and all realms of creation?

Recent conditions on Earth make it clear that humanity's misuse of natural resources has significantly altered climate and weather patterns on our planet, affecting all living beings—plants, animals and humans. Countless conferences and publications warn us daily of the dire environmental consequences of humanity's actions. If we conclude that humanity is the ultimate realm of creation because of its power of thought or reasoning, then humanity bears a great responsibility for its actions in the past and present and must immediately unify its thinking about a remedy. The preservation of humanity, as well as all living beings, depends on achieving this level of unity. Humanity can achieve this only through the uniquely human power of rational thought and unified action.

In some Scriptures, the Divine Educator who originally delivered the wisdom and guidance that we have come to call a "religion" is referred to as a "Manifestation of God," implying that His Teachings manifest the qualities of an Unknowable Essence.

> The well-being of mankind, its peace and security, are unattainable unless and until its unity is firmly established.[46]

> The knowledge of the Reality of the Divinity is impossible and unattainable, but the knowledge of the Manifestations of God (Moses, Christ, Mohammad, etc.) is the knowledge of God, for the bounties, splendors, and divine attributes are apparent in them. Therefore if man attains to the knowledge of the Manifestations of God, he will attain to the knowledge of God; and if he be neglectful of the knowledge of the Holy Manifestation, he will be bereft of the knowledge of God.[47]

These Divine Educators—these Manifestations of God—bring their council to the whole of humanity. Though they appear only in a specific highly populated area or where guidance is most needed, their Teachings are meant universally for all civilization, not just the population into which they were physically born or had a presence.

---

46 Bahá'u'lláh, *Gleanings from the Writings of Bahá'u'lláh*, CXXXI, p. 286
47 'Abdu'l-Bahá, *Some Answered Questions*, pp. 220-222.

Chapter 4:
Investigation of Truth

True Information

On any given topic, rational decisions require true information, or the best information available. If information contains flawed data or data based on feelings, the decisions based on it may also be flawed and can be detrimental to humanity. Thus, every decision requires accurate information and rational thinking to discern truth from falsehood.

Historically, religious ideology has been a major cause of irrational thinking. When theologians and religious authorities are not able to rationally defend their religious Scriptures, they often discourage logical thinking among believers and insist that they blindly accept and follow certain "truths" even when they conflict with proven scientific principles, sometimes on pain of death.

How do they do this? Parables meant simply to teach moral or spiritual concepts are claimed to be literally true in every aspect. In some cases, acceptance of religious beliefs that defy science have been praised as a hallmark of "true believers." This pervasive anti-intellectual mindset has taught humankind to disregard facts or reason in all aspects of religious, political, social and cultural inquiry.

Even today, in many quarters, the use of rational thought to evaluate the truth of things is scorned, in some cases even punished by imprisonment or death. An individual's beliefs and decisions are often manipulated by using the powerful emotions of fear, love and hate. True believers frequently adopt a sense of superiority over those who do not accept their beliefs. This establishes an exclusive caste of "us" versus "them" and has given rise to belittling labels for others such as "heathens," "gentiles" and "apostates."

These hardened attitudes, which result from what some analysts have called "the power of faith," have caused some faith-based groups to fall into a trap of their own making. When they cannot rationally explain a certain belief, they insist that true believers must blindly accept that belief on faith rather than rational thinking. Asking questions is frowned upon as the sign of a doubter. This behavior inevitably produces a culture of ignorance, which eventually leads to even more estrangement from non-believers. There are many examples today of religious sects that have segregated themselves so completely that they have arisen against each other, sometimes violently, to force their faith and decisions upon others and establish their superiority.

The powerful sway of religious leaders to undermine rational thinking is evident in terrorist organizations such as Al-Qaeda or the Nazi regime and its philosophy, in which directives from the leaders rely on the blind faith of their believers to kill and maim people, even commit acts of suicidal violence. This shows the destructive power of irrational thinking and the highest level of blind faith.

Such irrational and disunifying behavior can also be witnessed in politics. For example, the loyal supporter of a politician often encourages others to lend financial and moral support. Some people may agree with that enthusiastic supporter, but others may not. Depending on the candidate's character or platform, the new supporters will often find ways to show that their belief is sincere while those who rejected the candidate will try to prove that their rejection of the candidate was correct.

Because the support of both sides in such a political conflict is often based on emotions, facts eventually cease to play much of a role in the political discourse. Issues become clouded and heated. Supporters are exhorted to "do what you know is right" even when the rightness is irrational or unfounded. The divided political sides take up arms, either figuratively or literally, in a battle of wills that spills outside the boundaries of reason.

As history shows, when religious leaders expand their sphere of influence into the world of politics, the resulting disunity and conflict can envelop whole nations and lead to great wars and the suffering and death of thousands. When religious doctrines rely on blind faith, rational discussions become useless. The history of Hinduism, the ancient Hebrews, Christianity and Islam provides witness to the atrocities that humans can commit in the name of religion based on blind faith.

The bitter fruits of irrational thinking can be seen in almost all human endeavors. National boundaries have been drawn arbitrarily to separate one nation from another. Political groups have been created to separate people and cause them to distrust each other. Different interpretations of the same Holy Scriptures have split church congregations. When rational thinking is discouraged, one group often attempts to exalt itself above all others.

History has repeatedly shown the dangers that lurk when a religious community or political group emotionally chooses a leader believed to be the ultimate source of truth or to have divine powers, which can lead followers to see themselves as a chosen people because of their support. Social media in the twenty-first century has unfortunately handed a megaphone to anyone or any movement that wants to manipulate the blind faith of believers.

Sources of Information

Fact-checking, a cornerstone of rational thinking, requires more than consulting one's favored social media channels. Information on which we are going to base opinions or make decisions always needs to be critically evaluated to determine whether it is true or false. Understanding the source of the information is important. Is it a biased or unbiased source? Is the source promoting a product, idea or philosophy that is irrational? If so, it is not reliable.

Religious leaders, trusted politicians and financial advisors are usually considered unbiased and reliable sources of information. But are they really? Is the politician running for office and perhaps willing to slant the truth to expand his circle of supporters? Is the financial consultant benefiting from commissions for investment products? Is the religious leader an independent and rational thinker?

A high level of trust in a human source may be all that's needed for minor issues, but more important topics may require a deeper critique. Printed, broadcast and internet sources of information almost always need rational assessment and comparison to other sources. We carefully choose the best experts and alternative strategies we can find for financial planning, healthcare and building projects. Why, then, do we not look for the best rational explanations for the outcome of our religious beliefs and compare the information available from different wisdom traditions?

Such research can be hard work. A friend told one of the authors of this book, "I pay my minister to do this work and find the truth." But an independent search for truth is a requirement for personal spiritual development and a lifelong pursuit. It is so important that the first teaching of the Baha'í Faith, our newest wisdom tradition, is the duty for everyone to investigate reality. What does this mean?

> **It means that man must forget all hearsay and examine truth himself, for he does not know whether statements he hears are in accordance with reality or not. Wherever he finds truth or reality, he must hold to it, forsaking, discarding all else; for outside of reality there is naught but superstition and imagination...[48]**

---

48 'Abdu'l-Baha, *The Promulgation of Universal Peace*, p. 61.

In the field of religion, however, spiritual rewards about matters of faith are usually promised to be made manifest in the next world. This requires blind faith. In the hadith corpus, a Muslim male believer is promised seventy-two virgins in the next world if he unquestioningly does the bidding of a leader that leads to martyrdom.[49] No one seems to ask about the reward for a female believer in the next world. What part of this is rational? In the non-material, spiritual afterlife, how does providing seventy-two virgins that are supposedly for the believer's sexual gratification make any sense? Do souls engage in physical sex? A Christian woman believes she is promised a mansion on a street paved with gold in her afterlife if she accepts Jesus as her personal savior. What use does one's soul have for a physical mansion or gold?

Besides promising spiritual rewards, the main Teachings of every Divine Educator are rational and intended to promote the unification of humankind. The original Teachings, when they can be accessed, should be evaluated based on their own merits. Unfortunately, many of these teachings have been distorted into irrationality because of later misinterpretations.

It may be difficult, certainly impractical, to assess every new piece of information we encounter, but investigating the sources can help to determine the validity of the information itself. Rational thinking relies on information and knowledge acquired from credible, verifiable sources. A growing field of education is called media literacy and focuses on teaching the public how to discern between trustworthy and untrustworthy sources and between factual content and "fake news."

In this age of mass communications and social media, more and more channels of information are available to the public. Information on these channels is usually presented as true and unbiased. Unfortunately, not everything written is true and not everything said can be accepted at face value. Generally, unsolicited information is

---

49   Jamií al-Tirmidhi, 4:21:268.

the most suspect. Much "news" is merely hearsay or entertainment. Other information may sound more reputable, particularly when a presenter has academic credentials, but these credentials need to be examined too. Many readers will remember the case of Congressman George Santos who admitted lying about most of his personal history and resumé prior to his election in 2022.

A ceramic mug in a friend's kitchen contained this humorous saying: "I don't need Google. My mother knows everything." Undoubtedly this has many meanings, but it accurately reminds us that people are more likely to believe information from a source they trust not because it is correct, but because it makes them feel good or helps them meet their goal. Information from one's mother is based on a belief that a child, who grew up believing his mother was always right, accepts as truth. A child is not mature enough to think independently. But as adults, many of us still accept new ideas unthinkingly, like children. Perhaps it is time we matured enough to evaluate information based on our own reasoning, focus on the original Teachings and start making decisions for ourselves especially about spiritual matters.

As billions of messages bombard the public every day, the opportunities for biased or totally false information to be accepted as facts can lead to disastrous results. The standard for reporting by journalists is therefore of extreme importance. Interestingly, the youngest of the world's wisdom traditions directly addresses the responsibility of journalism.

> **The publication of high thoughts is the dynamic power in the arteries of life; it is the very soul of the world... Public opinion must be directed toward whatever is worthy of this day, and this is impossible except through the use of adequate arguments and the adducing of clear, comprehensive and conclusive proofs. For the helpless masses know nothing of the world, and while there is no doubt that they seek and long for their own**

happiness, yet ignorance like a heavy veil shuts them away from it...[50]

It has become ever more challenging to identify reputable and up-to-date sources of information. A strong desire to investigate truth and maintain an open mind about new information boosts confidence in decisions based on that information. Such decisions can promote unity and guide the progress of humanity.

> Knowledge is as wings to man's life, and a ladder for his ascent. Its acquisition is incumbent upon everyone. The knowledge of such sciences, however, should be acquired as can profit the peoples of the earth, and not those, which begin with words and end with words.[51]

Many wars have been fought due to a lack of reliable information or its misinterpretation by leaders who enjoy the trust of their followers. All wars are the result of irrational thinking usually based on national, political, racial or religious prejudices.

At this stage in the history of humanity, is it rational to believe that one person or one group is better than another? Such misguided beliefs seem to be ingrained in our very beings and cultures. We constantly assess our standing in society and calculate how much better we are than others. We constantly disregard the admonitions of the basic Teachings of the Holy Scriptures:

> Judge not, that ye be not judged.[52]

> Know ye not why We created you all from the same dust? That no one should exalt himself over the other.[53]

---

50 'Abdu'l-Bahá, *The Secret of Divine Civilization*.
51 Bahá'u'lláh, *Tablets of Bahá'u'lláh*, pp. 51-52.
52 *Bible*, Matthew 7:1 (King James version).
53 Bahá'u'lláh, *The Hidden Words of Bahá'u'lláh*, from the Arabic, No. 68.

Do we consider some people to be less successful because they drive small, inexpensive cars but hold in high regard others because they live in fancy houses and drive flashy automobiles? The truth is that without knowing another person well, we do not know if she is happy or sad, if he is productive to society or not, if she has new ideas that we can learn from or lacks creativity. We put value on possession of material assets but seldom on a person's character and thoughts. Through these flaws in rational thinking, we totally ignore the good counsel of Jesus: "Judge not, that ye be not judged." (Matthew 7:1) Instead, we consider ourselves to be authorities capable of judging one person or group against another.

From the perspective of rational thinking, this attitude of self-appointed authority is complete foolishness. It is based on misconceptions and blind imitation of the mindsets of others to support a false sense of superiority. It is a soul-killer, cutting us off from our noble, spiritual heritage and reinforcing our animal instincts. In the animal kingdom, only the strong and healthy survive. When we allow our thinking and behavior to be debased to the level of animal instincts, our social behaviors also decline, leading us to assert our superiority in many areas that may elevate our power over others, such as physical strength, beauty, intelligence, wealth, religious sect, race, citizenship and club membership. If we do not fit into a category preferred by our society, we lose status so others who possess such pre-conceived superiorities can dominate. Deep down, though, most of us know that every individual is a unique creation of God, and each person is important and valuable in this life.

Because our emotions and stubborn mental paradigms usually rule our self-perceived worth and status in society, material possessions often become our focus, setting us on the path to conflict, contention and even war. Although we recognize that the "reality of man is his thoughts," [54] we continually dwell on the material side of our being because, well… we can see material things but cannot see

---

54 'Abdu'l-Bahá, *Paris Talks*, p. 17-18.

anyone's thoughts.

In truth, however, the importance of each person exists in their service to others, not themselves. This is the basis for the oft-quoted goal for each person to be "a productive member of society."

Even though "the reality of man is his thoughts," in troubled times plagued by irrational thinking only individuals who submit to society's misguided standards are accepted. Others are unjustly pushed aside, with the excuse that this is necessary for the "survival of the fittest." As a result, the rational soul—our ability to think and reason—is neglected, and our limited time on Earth is wasted in the mere pursuit of material desires empty in their essence.

> First and foremost, among these favors which the Almighty hath conferred upon man, is the gift of understanding. His purpose in conferring such a gift is none other except to enable His creature to know and recognize the one true God—exalted be His glory. This gift giveth man the power to discern the truth in all things, leadeth him to that which is right, and helpeth him to discover the secrets of creation.[55]

All the Divine Educators have tried to teach us to be self-sacrificing and dedicated to the service of others. Why is it, then, that we continue to separate ourselves from others by associating with groups that enhance our own value in the social order but often exclude some others? When challenged by the injustice inherent in this type of thinking, we either have no response or defend our actions by claiming the need to ensure the survival of humanity based on the concept of "survival of the fittest," a standard for the animal kingdom, not humanity.

How is it that we have allowed ourselves to become so preoccupied with material things in these few precious days of our

---

55   Bahá'u'lláh, *Gleanings from the Writings of Bahá'u'lláh*, XCV, p. 194.

lives? Do we not realize that this life may end at any moment, and we will have to leave empty-handed into an unknown world?

> This gift [of understanding] giveth man the power to discern the truth in all things, leadeth him to that which is right, and helpeth him to discover the secrets of creation.[56]

The Problem of Certitude

Both science and religion—including philosophy—have a certitude problem. They often get ahead of themselves in making grand pronouncements of truth that become widely accepted as *absolute* truths.

Looking back on the ancient Greeks, we find sweeping statements made with great confidence about the nature of reality in the works of Plato and Aristotle. Plato presented the concept of a world of forms more real than the physical world, and Aristotle wrote in detail about the perfection and composition of the heavens.

A few hundred years later, a developing Christian tradition promoted with great confidence its new truths—that Jesus was God and performed miracles, and that sin was inherited. By the seventeenth century, however, many confident assertions were being challenged by diverse skeptics. Both the Catholic theological tradition and the Aristotelian scientific tradition (remember Christian reformer Martin Luther and astronomer Galileo?) were under assault and, lacking rational defenses, eventually eroded along with society's confidence in such previous sweeping statements. Philosophers started thinking harder about such basic questions as "How is it we know anything at all?"

Prominent philosophers, such as Descartes and Spinoza, traveled down the path of rationalism. Francis Bacon pursued an empirical track, and Immanuel Kant attempted to resolve their

---

56   Bahá'u'lláh, *Gleanings from the Writings of Bahá'u'lláh*, XCV, p. 194.

different approaches in a unique way. Kant's attempts to reduce this tension of ideas was eventually "nibbled away by skeptical termites," in the words of Dr. Karl Giberson, who holds a PhD in physics from Rice University and has lectured on science and religions at the Vatican, Oxford, MIT, Brigham Young and Xavier University. "… by the 20th century philosophers had essentially given up on finding out how we might actually come to know anything."[57]

Scientists largely avoided these discouraging and inconclusive debates. New sciences sprung up—astronomy, physics, geology, chemistry, biology, cosmology. According to Giberson:

> Each new science provided profound new insights into the world. Some of those insights —like "energy is always conserved in every interaction," or "the universe originated in a Big Bang 14 billion years ago"—had the same sort of sweeping scope as the pronouncements of Plato and Augustine. And that should be tossed, I suppose, on the ash heap, with Plato's Forms and Augustine's original sin, and yet they are not.[58]

How science has escaped the Philosophical Inquisition is a question even scientists cannot answer, perhaps because such philosophical questions are not a subject of conversation in scientific communities. One branch of science, however—medicine—provides some relevant clues.

Every day, thousands of people—many of them thoughtful, educated and even skeptical— submit to the promises of medical science to diagnose and heal their health issues. We allow them to

---

57   Dr. Karl Giberson, Rice University, from a talk documented at https://sinaiandsynapses.org/content/why-doubt-and-uncertainty-are-good-for-both-religion-and-science/.

58   Dr. Karl Giberson, Rice University, from a talk documented at https://sinaiandsynapses.org/content/why-doubt-and-uncertainty-are-good-for-both-religion-and-science/.

anesthetize us, which brings us perilously close to death—to open us up with scalpels, to inject us with all kinds of drugs and then restore our consciousness. By submitting to these intrusions, we acknowledge the reliability of medicine's scientific claims. We do this not based on blind faith, but on the record of past results and our knowledge of the rigor with which every procedure is done.

Science is not an end run around religion or philosophy but is the process of rational thinking and a method of acquiring knowledge about the world without always being able to explain what is observed or discovered. We recognize that science has learned important things about the world, and while sometimes we may not be able to explain how or justify those conclusions to critics, we don't have to. The result is the proof. It doesn't matter if the greatest chef understands the recipe; the pudding has made its own argument.

As we set out to acquire knowledge, we should consider some of the insights gained from a study of the history of science. Most people think that science is unrivaled in its rigor for finding truth, its obsession for understanding causes and effects, and its ability to collate data into useful information. Dr. Giberson has identified four surprising insights:

1. ***Science often moves forward with incomplete knowledge***. The science of mechanics, both celestial and terrestrial, dramatically proceeded forward for centuries with no concept of a central feature—gravity. "The quest for knowledge is compatible with deep mystery."

2. ***Science regularly confronts anomalies***. Countless observations have contradicted dominant scientific ideas. For example, the orbits of Mercury and Saturn were found to refute Newton's theory of gravity. The overall success of Newton's calculations, however, convinced the science community to ignore them. Apparently, the quest for knowledge is also compatible with the existence of inconsistencies.

3. ***Scientific tradition uses anomalies to move forward and discover new things***. A possible explanation for the odd behavior of Saturn was the gravitational pull of a possible undiscovered planet. When a telescope was aimed at the location where the new planet would need to be, Uranus was discovered. The quest for knowledge should be associated with progress.

4. ***Science is communal***. Scientific truths are not presented at the conclusion of experiments and observations but are announced at the end of scientific reviews by peers. Observations do not interpret themselves. The participants in peer reviews often have different types of expertise, all of which are required to bring the truth into focus.

In the religious sphere, what would happen if we simply accepted that the Bible was riddled with inconsistencies, as it clearly is, instead of spending time arguing about what cannot be defended? What if we reflected instead on the important lessons the Bible (and other Scriptures) have been telling us? What if all came to believe that, as in establishing scientific consensus, it does not matter along which path the devout students of religion have traveled to arrive at the same conclusions?

It is unfair to state our opinions as truth simply because we believe they are true. Our certitude is seldom persuasive. But when the collective wisdom of our diverse wisdom traditions converges on a point, we should pay attention. We may have found truth about something. It may not be absolute truth, however, for as knowledge increases, so does truth continue to unfold. And as world conditions evolve, so must what we hold to be true about the changing world.

Truth is Not Absolute

The Third Law of Thermodynamics teaches that the entropy of a system approaches a constant value as the temperature approaches absolute zero. In other words, the entropy of a perfect crystal at absolute zero is exactly equal to zero. At any temperature above absolute zero, entropy (or change) begins to occur. All things in the physical world, then, are either moving toward development or degradation unless they are at absolute zero. Nothing stays the same.

This is true of knowledge also. Rational thinking recognizes that knowledge is not absolute but relative. In other words, as more information becomes available about a topic, such as the cause of a disease or the effectiveness of a particular treatment, our understanding of those specific facts, as well as how they affect the entire world, must also progress. Truth, then, is relative to the time in which we live. What was the best "truth" before the cause of an illness was known must be replaced by a more informed "truth" as new and proven information becomes available, otherwise failed remedies based on the former flawed knowledge will continue to be used.

If religious truth is revealed to humanity by God in measures according to what society can understand at any particular time, then perhaps religious truth is also relative to the time in which we live. The tribal people in the Old Testament time of Abraham would not have understood some of Jesus's teachings and the need for revoking certain laws as he did. But the Roman society of Jesus's time had progressed to a more informed stage and was ready for His revelation of new teachings, which introduced the concept of a Divine Educator and Savior, Jesus.

Rational thinking is a tool that has led to many great advancements in the material world. For centuries, humans thought the earth was flat based on visual evidence. Eventually, it was proven by Greek, Chinese, Islamic and European scientists and philosophers that the information based on sight alone was incorrect. The developing disciplines of mathematics and astronomy proved that the earth is round. Today, no rational person disputes this fact.

The power of reason is the greatest endowment of all humans. It is the only reliable way to investigate true information.

> Know ye that God has created in man the power of reason, whereby man is enabled to investigate reality. God has not intended man to imitate blindly his fathers and ancestors. He has endowed him with mind, or the faculty of reasoning, by the exercise of which he is to investigate and discover the truth, and that which he finds real and true he must accept... The greatest cause of bereavement and disheartening in the world of humanity is ignorance based upon blind imitation. It is due to this that wars and battles prevail; from this cause hatred and animosity arise continually among mankind.[59]

All people through their own free wills must seek the truth even while understanding that when truth is found it may not be an *absolute* truth. Maintaining an ever-questioning, ever-learning attitude is essential because knowledge expands over time, and consequently truth evolves. Knowledge is infinite, and humanity will continually advance as its understanding of truth advances. So, truth is based on the knowledge we currently have of any topic at any time.

The desire to investigate truth is the best protection and guide for the well-being of humanity. The lack of progress in understanding truth is one way of initiating the death of a society or oneself. This is why deepening an understanding of truth is so essential and why the Holy Scriptures encourage an inquisitive and investigative mind. Christ advised His followers to...

> Ask, and it shall be given you; seek, and ye shall find; knock, and it shall be opened unto you.[60]

---

59   'Abdu'l-Bahá, *The Promulgation of Universal Peace*, p. 291.
60   *Bible*, Luke 11: 9

Later, a tradition in the revelation of Muhammad assured us that God would not abandon a seeker.

> Whoso seeketh Me shall find Me. Whoso findeth Me, shall be drawn towards Me. Whoso draweth nigh unto Me, shall love Me. Whoso loveth Me, him shall I also love. He who is beloved of Me, him shall I slay. He who is slain by Me, I Myself shall be his ransom.[61]

Faith and the Scientific Process

Many actions in our daily lives are taken because we have faith that is based on past experience and reasoning. For example, we have faith that the sun will rise every day and set at a certain time. This faith is based on past experience and, unless we drastically change our location on the planet, this could be considered conscious knowledge or rational faith.

Past experience and experiments are the basis of the scientific process. Researchers carefully plan and carry out experiments, gather as much experimental and provable data as possible to verify the results, and then share their assumptions, findings and conclusions with other scientists in their field of study. It is understood that assumptions do not carry the same weight as established data or facts. In a well-structured system of peer review, a study and its conclusions are published in an accepted scientific publication. Other scientists then have an opportunity to verify or challenge any part of the experiment or its results. In many cases, reviewers offer alternative conclusions and theories.

Science requires a degree of humility. Each researcher can only offer his or her limited understanding and must accept that these findings do not have any final authority. A scientist must always be open to the discovery of errors or misunderstandings. This view of

---

61   Nabil, *The Dawn-Breakers: Nabil's Narrative of the Early Days of the Baha'i Revelation*, Pages 47-97: 72

knowledge keeps doors open to further debate with peers and the hope that more knowledge can be gained through consultation. Without such humility, scientific research would have no credibility.

Because knowledge is infinite, we can never know everything. Whether it is knowledge of science or of religious concepts or divinity, there will always be more to learn. If this focus of gathering information and knowledge is spent in the betterment of humankind, it is then acceptable and worthy. Otherwise it is a waste of time and can be misguided.

> There are certain pillars which have been established as the unshakeable supports of the Faith of God. The mightiest of these is learning and the use of the mind, the expansion of consciousness, and insight into the realities of the universe and the hidden mysteries of Almighty God.[62]

> Blessed and happy is he that ariseth to promote the best interests of the peoples and kindreds of the earth.... It is not for him to pride himself who loveth his own country, but rather for him who loveth the whole world. The earth is but one country, and mankind its citizens.[63]

Faith and Wisdom

Rational thinking and faith are interconnected, eventually leading to wisdom. What exactly is wisdom? The human mind, being a part of the human realm, cannot comprehend the infinite. Humans can only understand things in relation to other things known from experience. As examples, a person's physical appearance, skin color or intelligence are all descriptions that are relative to someone else.

---

62 'Abdu'l-Bahá, *Selections from the Writings of 'Abdu'l-Bahá*, #97, p. 126.
63 Bahá'u'lláh, *Gleanings from the Writings of Bahá'u'lláh*, CXVII, p. 250.

For example, if someone is described as tall, that person's height is relative to the height of others. It can be challenging for anyone to understand the experiences of a new culture because much of our knowledge is relative to our past experiences.

The human soul—with its power of thought, reasoning and understanding—is the greatest means we have to develop our full potentials and acquire heavenly attributes or virtues. Faith based on experience or rational thought, which we may call "rational faith," encourages humans to explore the unknown. Wisdom develops when both rational thinking and rational faith combine to assist in making good decisions and evaluating the outcome of those decisions. Wisdom is the melding of knowledge with insight, which is an ability to discern inner qualities and relationships that can help predict future outcomes.

As humanity looks to the future, we must also reflect on the lessons of history and rely on rational thinking and rational faith to gain greater wisdom and keener insight for the future. Only then can we hope to safeguard the future of humanity.

> The past is the mirror of the future. Gaze ye therein and be apprised thereof…. In this day the choicest fruit of the tree of knowledge is that which serveth the welfare of humanity and safeguardeth its interests.[64]

Humanity is in desperate need of wisdom. To achieve this goal, decisions affecting the future of humanity must be based on an evaluation of the errors of the past. Rational faith can inspire the courageous actions of individuals and governments to move forward with confidence and resolve as they begin to tackle seemingly impossible problems.

After observing the decay of mainstream organized religions, many people have grown disenchanted with past belief systems. Instead, they choose to become agnostics, atheists or naturalists. Some

---

64 Bahá'u'lláh, *The Tabernacle of Unity*, paragraphs 1.14-1.16.

replace religious beliefs with belief in other systems or adherence to political or socio-economic causes. But is that possibly "throwing the baby out with the bath water?"

Faith and Belief

Most of the world's religions have established structured statements of faith and belief to which believers are required to pledge allegiance as a condition of becoming a member of that religion. Statements of faith and belief can be classified into two categories—one based on knowledge and wisdom gained from experimentation, observation, and experience; the other based primarily on acceptance of authoritative opinions or the believer's own feelings, particularly the subjective sense of what is right or true.

Many existing statements of faith are of the latter type, which aptly describes the concept of "blind faith." The opinions of theologians and clergy become highly influential when the believer decides that interpretation of the Scriptures has been awarded to only one, or perhaps a few, chosen persons within a religious organization. These anointed leaders come to believe, or at least to claim, that they are divinely inspired and therefore their opinions are infallible, or nearly so. Believers who agree with the statement of faith are obliged to follow the directives of these leaders and are discouraged from questioning the authority figures. In the Jewish, Christian and Islamic faiths, individuals of all backgrounds can enter religious schools of faith and receive a diploma that grants them enormous authority in the name of God. Where did such a concept come from?

Examples of authoritarian religious leaders can be found throughout history and around the world. Examples include: ancient Chinese emperors; Babylonian kings; Egyptian pharaohs; Aztec kings and priests who promoted human sacrifice as a religious ritual; and seventeenth-century Roman Catholic popes who persecuted and imprisoned the scientists and mathematicians whose scientific discoveries differed from Church doctrine.

In our time, however, as the world's overall educational level improves, younger members of society are more likely to evaluate and question statements of faith and belief. They are less inclined to blindly yield to authority, particularly if their questions are not adequately answered or the answers are not logical or reasonable. Longstanding and irrational explanations of religious truth have caused many people to give up on religion. When asked, many "people of faith" express ignorance of the teachings of their religious Scriptures, a confession of sorts to the blindness of their faith.

> The vitality of belief in God is dying out in every land; nothing short of God's wholesome medicine can ever restore it. The corrosion of ungodliness is eating into the vitals of human society; what else but the Elixir of His potent Revelation can cleanse and revive it? ... The Word of God, alone, can claim the distinction of being endowed with the capacity required for so great and far-reaching a change.[65]

While the power of religion may be diminishing in many lands, in others the grip of religious fanaticism and superstition is tightening. In numerous nations the government's constitution and laws are based on the teachings and traditions of a specific religion. As a result, some nations perpetuate such outdated standards for belief and behavior that the unity and progress of their societies have been destroyed. A current example of this destruction is occurring in the Islamic Republic of Iran as its fundamentalist regime uses a secret police force to enforce the edicts of the Supreme Leader. This and all repressive conduct is contrary to spiritual truth.

In the early 1800s, inflamed by his perceived abuses by religions of all kinds, a deist named Elihu Palmer penned these words:

---

65   Bahá'u'lláh, *Gleanings from the Writings of Bahá'u'lláh*, XCIX, p. 200.

There is a science, that has for its object only things incomprehensible. Contrary to all other sciences, it treats only of what cannot fall under our senses... It is a country, where everything is governed by laws contrary to those which mankind are permitted to know in the world they inhabit. In this marvelous region, light is only darkness; evidence is doubtful or false; impossibilities are credible; reason is a deceitful guide; and good sense becomes madness. This science is called theology, and this sort of theology is a continual insult to the reason of man.[66]

These are strong words conveyed emotionally, but even today they summarize how many people view religion. Is he right in his convictions? Is religion too often a dark force rather than a source of light? Has religion been hijacked by its priesthood and theologians?

This day the powers of all the leaders of religion are directed towards the dispersion of the congregation of the All-Merciful, and the shattering of the Divine Edifice. The hosts of the world, whether material, cultural or political are from every side launching their assault...[67]

As religious-based governmental oppression is on the rise, many new religious sects are splintering away from their co-religionist roots due to conflicting interpretations of Scriptures and disputes over how to organize their religious communities. Many of these different viewpoints are based on emotions and feelings rather than knowledge and wisdom gained from observation and experience. Blind emotional commitment to an interpretation of Writings deemed holy often leads to prejudice and fanaticism. It is seldom the

66   https://www.gutenberg.org/files/7319/7319-h/7319-h.htm.
67   'Abdu'l-Bahá, quoted in Shoghi Effendi, *The Advent of Divine Justice*, p. 5

religion itself but rather the way it is used to coerce and manipulate society that is at fault.

Yet we again see that the promises of the Divine Educators deviate from our present logical explanations by asking for purity of heart and motive and a true desire to become aware of the spiritual knowledge available to us. It makes everyone the judge of his or her own conclusions and gives no credence to the judgements of others. How responsible and freeing is this concept of self-evaluation?

Whether it is knowledge of science or knowledge of religious concepts or divinity, there will always be more to learn. If this focus of gathering information and knowledge is spent in the betterment of humankind, it is then acceptable and worthy, otherwise it is a waste of time and easily can be misguided. In the writings of the Bahá'í Faith, we find the following statement from the mouthpiece of the Divine:

> In this Day therefore I bear witness unto My creatures, for the witness of no one other than Myself hath been or shall ever be worthy of mention in My presence. I affirm that no Paradise is more sublime for My creatures than to stand before My face and to believe in My holy Words, while no fire hath been or will be fiercer for them than to be veiled from the Manifestation of My exalted Self and to disbelieve in My Words.[68]

And in the Writings of the Baha'i Faith, it is written:

> Some lamented in their separation from Me, others endured hardships in My path, and still others laid down their lives for the sake of My Beauty, could ye but know it. Say: I, verily, have not sought to extol Mine own Self, but rather God Himself, were ye to judge fairly. Naught can be seen in Me except God and His Cause, could

---

68 The Báb, *Selections from the Writings of the Báb*, pp. 87-88

ye but perceive it. I am the One Whom the tongue of Isaiah hath extolled, the One with Whose name both the Torah and the Evangel were adorned. Thus hath it been decreed in the Scriptures of thy Lord, the Most Merciful. He, verily, hath borne witness unto Me, as I bear witness unto Him. And God testifieth to the truth of My words.[69]

---

69 Bahá'u'lláh, *The Summons of the Lord of Hosts*, pp. 83-88

Chapter 5:
Redefining Religion

Definition of Religion

In the broadest sense, religion can be defined as a person's relationship with the Creator and from the earliest days was intended to be a source of unity. Being so private, how did religion then become a social arena for segregating people based on the differences in this relationship?

Over time, religion has evolved and with it the various ways in which people show devotion to God such as worship and prayer, moral conduct and adhering to righteous beliefs and religious rituals within a given society.

Religion is more narrowly understood by many, however, to mean a set of religious teachings and practices that are associated with the Holy Scriptures revealed by one of the Divine Educators such as Krishna in Hinduism, Buddha in Buddhism, Moses in the Jewish Faith, Jesus Christ in Christianity or Muhammad in Islam.

This narrow understanding of religion tends to focus on the differences in practices and rituals, which unfortunately encourages separation amongst the followers of different Educators. This also leads to confusion about the meaning of "religion" and creates the false impression that the revelation delivered by one Divine

Educator competes with all others for believers and derives from a different source. This is why many Christians believe that Islam is an invention of humans (or possibly Satan) that tricks believers into worshipping a false god, Allah, which is simply the Arabic word for God. It is why Muslims see some Christian beliefs as a sacrilege, an inversion of the true understanding of the Creator. They disagree with Christians who they believe blasphemously claim Jesus is the son of God and display idols representing Christ on a cross.

A deep study of the Holy Scriptures of all the wisdom traditions, however, reveals an essential unity. Though delivered at different times to disparate societies with distinctly varied cultures, these wisdom traditions have the same spiritual teachings such as belief in God, existence of the human soul, an exhortation to love our neighbors, to be honest, loyal and faithful. Only the material teachings—those related to the practices of daily life—differ in response to the time and conditions of the place in which those teachings were revealed.

> Religion... is not a series of beliefs, a set of customs; religion is the teachings of the Lord God, teachings which constitute the very life of humankind, which urge high thoughts upon the mind, refine the character, and lay the groundwork for man's everlasting honor.[70]

And yet as each new Revelation of wisdom has been introduced to humanity, it has been fiercely attacked by adherents of the "old ways" with the Educator severely persecuted, abused, exiled, imprisoned or murdered. The inevitable good that is promised in the new Revelation is ignored or disbelieved despite the elegant explanations provided by the Messengers. Is this rational? Should new information not be logically considered?

---

70   'Abdu'l-Bahá, *Selections from the Writings of 'Abdu'l-Bahá.* #23, pp. 52-53.

The Peril of New Paradigms

To better understand why humankind is so enthusiastically resistant to new religions, we can find a possible explanation in the work of Thomas S. Kuhn, a scientific historian and the author of *The Structure of Scientific Revolution*. Kuhn was one of the first to identify the impact of paradigms on the thought process, and in our opinion erred only in believing that paradigms were limited to the scientific world in which precise measurement and rigid control standards exist. He wrote that scientific paradigms…

> …are accepted examples of actual scientific practice, examples which include law, theory, application, and instrumentation together—[that] provide models from which spring particular coherent traditions of scientific research.

He added that…

> Men whose research is based on shared paradigms are committed to the same rules and standards for scientific practice.

A paradigm is the way we perceive the world. To a fish, the world is water. To many Christians, all other religions are heresies. When we are in the middle of the paradigm, it is hard to imagine any other.

The Jews alive during the time of Jesus were in the middle of a paradigm we now call Judaism and could not imagine any other. Christians in the time of Muhammad were trapped in a paradigm we call Christianity and were blind to any new thinking.

William Harmon, a key leader at the Stanford Research Institute, wrote in *An Incomplete Guide to the Future* that a paradigm is…

> …the basic way of perceiving, thinking, valuing, and doing associated with a particular vision of reality. A

> **dominant paradigm is seldom if ever stated explicitly; it exists unquestioned, tacit understanding that is transmitted through culture and to succeeding generations through direct experience rather than being taught.**

We know that most people who are raised in a religious tradition seldom depart from it entirely. Another term for the "unquestioned" nature of paradigms to which Harmon refers is "blind faith."

Joel Arthur Barker, in his groundbreaking book *Paradigms: The Business of Discovering the Future*, offered a practical definition:

> **A paradigm is a set of rules and regulations (written or unwritten) that does two things: (1) it establishes or defines boundaries; and (2) it tells you how to behave inside the boundaries in order to be successful.**

To illustrate the power of a paradigm to hold captive even the brightest minds, Barker begins his book with a true story that began in 1968. In that year, if anyone had been asked what nation would dominate the world of watchmaking in 1990, most would have replied, "Switzerland." After all, Switzerland had been the center of the watchmaking universe for over sixty years.

The Swiss made the best watches in the world and were famous for continuous improvements. They had invented the minute hand and the second hand. They had invested heavily in developing better ways to manufacture and configure the gears, bearings and mainsprings. They were not just resting on their laurels—they wanted to widen the leadership gap between Swiss-made watches and all others.

By 1968, the Switzerland watch industry had over 65 percent of the unit sales of watches and earned more than 80 percent of the profits (some analysts say 90 percent.) No one was even a close second. Within twelve years, however, their share of the market had fallen to less than 10 percent, and their profit domination plummeted to less than 20 percent.

Suddenly, the Swiss had run into a paradigm shift that they refused to acknowledge until it was too late. Stuck in the paradigm of mechanical watches made of gears and bearings and mainsprings, the Swiss stubbornly resisted predictable change as electronic watches took the world by storm. Between 1979 and 1981, fifty thousand Swiss watchmakers out of sixty-two thousand had lost their jobs. In a small country like Switzerland, this was a catastrophe.

Even more astonishing is that the Swiss themselves had invented the electronic quartz movement at their research institute in Neuchâtel, Switzerland. When the researchers presented this innovation to watch manufacturers in 1967, it was soundly rejected. After all, it had no mainspring. It required no bearings and almost no gears. It was battery-powered and electronic—barely resembling a watch at all except for its function of showing the correct time.

The researchers were allowed, however, to show off their useless innovation at the World Watch Congress that year. At the time, Japan had only about 1 percent of the watch market. Recognizing the enormous opportunity, the Japanese electronics firm Seiko took one look and, unbound by any watchmaking paradigm, immediately saw the future. The rest is history.

There are two perils of new paradigms. The first is suffered by whomever introduces the new paradigm and meets overwhelming disbelief and opposition. In the case of new wisdom traditions, response has usually been scorn, ridicule, vicious condemnation and often violence. It is astonishing that despite continuous threats and even wars to protect the "old ways," countless people eventually found value in the new teachings.

The second peril is suffered by those who reject the new paradigm because they forfeit the benefits that could have been theirs had they accepted the new way of thinking.

The human soul—with its power of thought, reasoning and understanding—is the greatest means to enable humans to develop their full potential and acquire heavenly attributes or virtues.

Rational faith encourages humans to explore the unknown. Wisdom develops when both rational thinking and rational faith combine to assist in making good decisions and evaluating the outcome of those decisions. Wisdom is the crucible of knowledge gained from experience or empirical data combined with insight, which is an ability to discern inner qualities and relationships that can help predict future outcomes.

As humanity looks to the future, we must also reflect on the lessons of history and rely on rational thinking and rational faith to gain greater wisdom for the future and escape our dysfunctional paradigms. Only then can we hope to safeguard the future of humanity.

> Say: O ye that have eyes to see! The past is the mirror of the future. Gaze ye therein and be apprised thereof…. In this day the choicest fruit of the tree of knowledge is that which serveth the welfare of humanity and safeguardeth its interests.[71]

Progressive Revelation

The history of religion shows that roughly every thousand years a Messenger, also called a Manifestation of God, has received knowledge from the Creator in a unique way and was made manifest in the world of humanity to provide guidance. The Revelation of God to Moses, for example, came as the voice of God speaking from a burning bush to reveal the Ten Commandments.[72] The Revelation to Christ was likened in the New Testament to a dove descending from heaven.[73] Muhammad described receiving his Revelation from the angel Gabriel, who commanded him to proclaim and read. The most recent Revelation came to Baha'u'llah in 1853 while he was

---

71   Bahá'u'lláh, *The Tabernacle of Unity,* paragraphs 1.14-1.16.
72   *Bible*, Exodus 3:4-6; 20, 24
73   *Bible*, Mathew 3:16; Mark 1:10; Luke 3: 22; John 1: 32

imprisoned for his teachings promoting world unity. He described this experience in these words:

> I was but a man like others, ... when lo, the breezes of the All-Glorious were wafted over Me, and taught Me the knowledge of all that hath been. This thing is not from Me, but from One Who is Almighty and All-Knowing. And He bade Me lift up My voice between earth and heaven, and for this there befell Me what hath caused the tears of every man of understanding to flow.[74]

A useful analogy that explains the relationship of God to humanity compares God with the sun and the Messengers of God with rays of the sun. Like God, the sun is our source of life. We cannot look directly at the light of the sun because of its intensity, but we can look at the rays of the sun, which bring us life-giving light and warmth. Similarly, we cannot fully understand the nature of the Divine, but we can learn about the Divine from the Holy Scriptures, God's Revelations, which were delivered to us by His Messengers. It is by studying these messages and observing the examples set by the Messengers that we can learn about the Divine.

> Men at all times and under all conditions stand in need of one to exhort them, guide them and to instruct and teach them. Therefore He (God) hath sent forth His Messengers, His Prophets and chosen ones that they might acquaint the people with the divine purpose underlying the revelation of Books and the raising up of Messengers, and that everyone may become aware of the trust of God which is latent in the reality of every soul.[75]

---

74 Bahá'u'lláh, *Epistle to the Son of the Wolf*, p. 11.
75 Bahá'u'lláh *Tablets of Bahá'u'lláh*, p. 156, 161.

Throughout history, according to the concept of progressive revelation, many Messengers have been chosen to reveal the Word of God.

> God hath raised up Prophets and revealed Books as numerous as the creatures of the world, and will continue to do so to everlasting.[76]

The history and teachings of several Messengers who appeared over the last 3,500 years are better known than their predecessors because the Holy Scriptures they revealed were written down and preserved. Each of these Messengers appeared in the world of humanity at a different time and place, but all of them have acknowledged the Messengers who appeared before them and have promised that a future Messenger would come to reveal even greater knowledge for the development of humanity.

According to our most recent wisdom tradition, these Messengers…

> …have been sent down from time immemorial, and been commissioned to summon mankind to the one true God. That the names of some of them are forgotten and the records of their lives lost is to be attributed to the disturbances and changes that have overtaken the world.[77]

In metaphoric language, the Old Testament identifies the first Manifestation as Adam, a subsequent Manifestation as Noah, and another as Abraham. The Bible continues to describe a succession of Manifestations from Moses (the Lawgiver) and Jesus (the Messiah). In veiled language it refers to future Manifestations, among them Muhammad (the Apostle of God), the Báb (the Point of the Bayán)

---

76 The Báb, *Selections from the Writings of The Báb*, p. 125.
77 Bahá'u'lláh, *Gleanings from the Writings of Bahá'u'lláh*, LXXXVII

and Bahá'u'lláh (Him Whom God shall make manifest). That these Manifestions were one and the same, though appearing at different times, was clearly proclaimed by the Apostle of God (Muhammad) when He knowingly proclaimed...

> I am all the Prophets, inasmuch as what shineth resplendent in each one of Them hath been and will ever remain the one and the same sun.[78]

Each body of knowledge delivered by a Manifestation of God (sometimes called a Divine Educator because of His primary role) is like a new chapter in the never-ending Holy Book of God's religion. Each chapter is not a new book but an expansion of the message that renews the spiritual teachings of the past and adds additional guidance for humanity as appropriate for the time in which it is revealed. Compare, for example, the spiritual teaching called the Golden Rule, which was expressed by several Messengers of God. From the Holy Scriptures revealed by Krishna in ancient India before 1300 BC:

> This is the sum of duty: do naught unto others which would cause you pain if done to you.[79]

From the Holy Scriptures revealed by Moses about 1200 BC:

> What is hateful to you, do not to your fellow man. That is the entire Law; all the rest is commentary.[80]

From the Buddha in India about 560 BC:

> Hurt not others in ways that you yourself would find hurtful.[81]

---

78   The Báb, *Selections from the Writings of The Báb*, p. 126.
79   Mahabharata 5 1517, from the Vedic tradition of India.
80   The Elder Hillel in Babylonian Talmud, Shabbat 31a
81   *Tibetan Dhammapada*, Udanavargu 5:18, 1983.

From the Scriptures revealed by Jesus in Israel about 30 AD:

> So in everything, do to others what you would have them do to you, for this sums up the Law and the Prophets.[82]

From the Holy Scriptures revealed by Muhammad in Arabia about 620 AD:

> The Prophet said, "No one of you is a believer until he desires for his brother that which he desires for himself."[83]

From the Bahá'í Faith in the 19th century:

> And if thine eyes be turned towards justice, choose thou for thy neighbor that which thou choosest for thyself.[84]

The essence of this spiritual truth is the same in all revelations, as this guidance has always come from the same divine source. Regarding other teachings on daily life, religious truth as revealed is not absolute but relative to the needs of humanity and its capacity to understand the new guidance. God's religion continues to be more fully revealed with the appearance of each new Educator. Through this pattern of progressive revelation, the religion of God will continue to provide more advanced guidance for the spiritual and material development of humanity.

Because of the common Source of inspiration, the Holy Scriptures revealed throughout history by the Manifestations of God have more similarities than differences. Unfortunately, the clergy and followers of each new revelation have often mistakenly perceived

---

82   *Bible*, Matthew 7:12,.
83   Riyad as-Salihin 236, Introduction, Hadith 236
84   Bahá'u'lláh, *Tablets of Bahá'u'lláh*, p. 64.

the Prophet-Founder of their accepted religion and its teachings to be superior to all others. Such attitudes have created rivalries with previous faith communities. There can be little religious discourse between these communities when each believes that its Messenger is the final Messenger, the "beginning" and the "end" of God's revelation to humanity, the "first" and the "last," the "alpha" and "omega."[85] Instead of anticipating a new Messenger, they await the "return" of their own Messenger, failing to understand that each New Messenger is the return of all the previous Ones.

The concept of progressive revelation asserts that while all of God's Messengers have complete knowledge, they are only allowed to reveal what is appropriate for the needs of the people at the time of the new revelation. With greater insight, scriptural language referring to the "beginning" and the "end" or the "first" and the "last" could be understood as describing how new guidance from each Messenger is the "beginning" of a new period of humanity's history and during that time is the new spiritual standard until another Messenger appears. The new guidance, then, is the same in the "beginning" of that period and until the "end" of that time.

Jesus proclaimed:

> I am the way, the truth, and the life: no man cometh unto the Father, but by me."[86]

This statement clearly explained that the new revelation He had brought to humanity was to be the standard for that time—that it renewed and clarified past revelations delivered by Abraham and Moses. But Jesus also promised that more guidance would be revealed in the future when He said:

---

85 Alpha and omega are the first and last letters of the Greek alphabet, the original language used to write down the New Testament. The meaning is therefore the same as "the first and the last." These letters were used to symbolize both God and Christ by some of the earliest Christian churches.

86 *Bible*, John 14:6.

> I have yet many things to say unto you, but ye cannot bear them now. Howbeit when he, the Spirit of Truth, is come, he will guide you into all truth."[87]

Some six hundred years later, Muhammad, the Messenger for the people of Arabia, proclaimed:

> Muhammad is not the father of [any] one of your men, but [he is] the Messenger of Allah and last of the prophets. And ever is Allah , of all things, Knowing.[88]

> We indeed sent many Messengers before you... Every age has its own [revealed] Book. [89]

> And call to mind, (O Prophet), when We took the covenant from all Prophets; and also from you and Noah and Abraham, Moses, and Jesus the son of Mary...[90]

Why do people need to declare that their beliefs are better than those of another person? Are they trying to show that they are special or better than others? Do they feel they have been "chosen" and will be "saved" while others who reject their beliefs are doomed? It seems childish to claim to be a parent's favorite child and entitled to greater rewards than other siblings when a good parent loves all of his children equally.

> Know thou assuredly that the essence of all the Prophets of God is one and the same. Their unity is absolute. God, the Creator, saith: There is no distinction whatso-

---

87 *Bible,* John 16: 12-13.
88 *Qur'án,* Surah 33: 40
89 *Qur'án,* Surah 13: 38-39
90 *Qur'án,* Surah 33:7-8

> ever among the Bearers of My Message. They all have but one purpose; their secret is the same secret. To prefer one in honor to another, to exalt certain ones above the rest, is in no wise to be permitted. Every true Prophet hath regarded His Message as fundamentally the same as the Revelation of every other Prophet gone before Him.[91]

Regrettably, rivalries between religions have often been the cause of great disunity, leading to cataclysmic wars. But the Holy Scriptures hold out an optimistic view of a more sane and peaceful society. The Old Testament prophet Isaiah foretold the conditions of days to come and promised the coming of a unified world.

> For I know their works and their thoughts: it shall come, that I will gather all nations and tongues; and they shall come, and see my glory.[92]

The most recent Messenger has specifically referred to the promises of Isaiah and proclaimed that our time is this day when all nations and tongues are being gathered together to establish the unity of humanity.

> Bend your minds and wills to the education of the peoples and kindreds of the earth, that haply the dissensions that divide it may... be blotted out from its face, and all mankind become the upholders of one Order, and the inhabitants of one City... Ye dwell in one world, and have been created through the operation of one Will. Blessed is he who mingleth with all men in a spirit of utmost kindliness and love.[93]

---

91 Bahá'u'lláh, *Gleanings from the Writings of Bahá'u'lláh*, XXXIV, pp. 78-79.
92 *Bible*, Isaiah 66:18.
93 Bahá'u'lláh, *Gleanings from the Writings of Bahá'u'lláh*, CLVI, pp. 333-334.

> In this wondrous Revelation, this glorious century, the foundation of the Faith of God, and the distinguishing feature of His Law, is the consciousness of the oneness of mankind.[94]

Succession Planning

Every Divine Educator has established a covenant or contract with humanity. An important part of this covenant is a promise that more guidance will come in the future to be delivered by a new Messenger, a "Promised One." From the Holy Scriptures revealed by Krishna, we are told that...

> Whenever there is decay of righteousness ... and there is exaltation of unrighteousness, then I Myself come forth; for the protection of the good, for the destruction of evil-doers, for the sake of firmly establishing righteousness. I am born from age to age.[95]

Moses, who established a Jewish civilization based on the Ten Commandments, promised that God would continue to honor His covenant with the Jewish people by sending more Prophets in the future.

> The Lord thy God will raise up unto thee a Prophet from the midst of thee, of thy brethren, like unto me; unto him ye shall hearken...[96]

Isaiah was one of the Prophets promised by Moses. In turn, Isaiah foretold the coming of a Promised One.

---

94 Shoghi Effendi, *The Promised Day is Come*, p. 123-124.

95 *Bhagavad Gita*, Fourth Discourse, cited in Ferraby, *All Things Made New*, p. 170.

96 *Bible*, Deuteronomy 18:15.

> For unto us a child is born, unto us a son is given: and the government shall be upon his shoulder: and his name shall be called Wonderful, Counsellor, The mighty God, The everlasting Father, The Prince of Peace. Of the increase of his government and peace there shall be no end, upon the throne of David, and upon his kingdom, to order it, and to establish it with judgment and with justice from henceforth even for ever.[97]

From the Holy Scriptures revealed by Zoroaster, we learn that...

> When a thousand two hundred and some years have passed from the inception of the religion of Abraham and the overthrow of the Kingdom of Iran and the degradation of the followers of My religion, a descendant of the Iranian King will be raised up as a Prophet, and His name shall be Sháh-Bahram. [98]

In the Writings of Buddha, we are told...

> I am not the first Buddha who came upon earth, nor shall I be the last. In due time another Buddha will rise in the world, a Holy One, a supremely enlightened One, endowed with wisdom in conduct, auspicious, knowing the universe, an incomparable leader of men, a master of angels and mortals. He will reveal to you the same eternal truths which I have taught you. He will preach his religion, glorious at the goal, in the spirit and in the letter. He will proclaim a religious life, wholly perfect and pure, such as I now proclaim... At this period, brethren, there will arise in the world an exalted One named Maitreye, Arahant, Fully Awakened, abounding

---

97   *Bible*, Isaiah, 9: 6-7.

98   Dinkird, late collection of Zoroastrian Holy Scriptures, cited in Ferraby, *All Things Made New*, p. 174.

> in wisdom and goodness, happy with knowledge of the worlds, unsurpassed as a guide to mortals willing to be led, a teacher for gods and men, an Exalted One, a Buddha, even as I am now… The truth. Lovely in its origin, lovely in its progress, lovely in its consummation, will he proclaim, both in the spirit and in the letter, the higher life will he make known, in all its fullness and in all its purity, even as I do now.[99]

Jesus affirmed this same promise numerous times.

> And other sheep I have, which are not of this fold: them also I must bring, and they shall hear my voice; and there shall be one fold, and one shepherd.[100]

> And this gospel of the kingdom shall be preached in all the world for a witness unto all nations; and then shall the end come.[101]

> For as the lightning cometh out of the east, and shineth even unto the west; so shall also the coming of the Son of man be.[102]

> …I go away, and come again unto you.[103]

> …when the Comforter is come… he shall testify of me.[104]

---

99   Buddha, as cited in Digha Nikaya, XCVI, p. 245; III, p. 75-76.
100 *Bible*, John 10:16.
101 *Bible*, Mathew 24:14.
102 *Bible*, Mathew 24: 26-27.
103 *Bible*, John 14:28
104 *Bible*, John 15:26

> I have yet many things to say unto you, but ye cannot bear them now. Howbeit when he, the Spirit of truth, is come, he will guide you into all truth."[105]

Also in the New Testament, the Apostle Paul expressed the hopes of the early Christians for the return or "coming of our Lord Jesus Christ" in one of his letters to the church at Corinth.

> For we know in part, and we prophesy in part. But when that which is perfect is come, then that which is in part shall be done away. When I was a child, I spake as a child, I understood as a child, I thought as a child: but when I became a man, I put away childish things. For now we see through a glass, darkly; but then face to face: now I know in part; but then shall I know even as also I am known.[106]

And in John's Revelation, it is recorded that when the spirit of Christ comes again...

> ...I will write upon him my new name.[107]

Echoing this promise to humankind, Muhammad calls himself the "Warner" of that Day… when "Our Lord will gather us together," the "Day of return" of the One Who Ariseth (the Qa'im) and the One Who is guided (the Mihdi). And then he affirms that...

> For every Message is a limit of time, and soon shall ye know it.[108]

---

105 *Bible*, John 16:12-13
106 *Bible*, 1 Corinthians 1: 7, 13: 9-12.
107 *Bible*, Revelation 3:12.
108 *Qur'án*, Surah 6:67.

> One day, the disturbing-trumpet blast shall disturb it, which the second blast shall follow. ...Verily, it will be but a single blast.[109]

> But if ye lapse after that our clear signs have come to you, know that God is Mighty, Wise. What can such expect but that God should come down to them overshadowed with clouds, and the angels also, and their doom be sealed? And to God shall all things return.[110]

The Messenger of God known as The Báb, a title meaning "The Gate," was imprisoned, put on trial and finally executed in 1850 by order of the religious leaders of Shí'ah Islam in Iran. When the Báb—who was the Forerunner of Bahá'u'lláh, the Prophet-Founder of the Bahá'í Faith—was asked during his trial to state who he claimed to be for the Shí'ah, He proclaimed...

> I am, I am, I am the promised One! I am the One whose name you have for a thousand years invoked, at whose mention you have risen, whose advent you have longed to witness, and the hour of whose Revelation you have prayed God to hasten. Verily I say, it is incumbent upon the peoples of both the East and the West to obey My word and to pledge allegiance to My person.[111]

The Scriptures revealed by The Báb demonstrate His unique role to reveal new guidance from God and prepare humanity for the coming of the long-awaited Promised One prophesied by all the revelations of the past. The Báb's brief ministry was like a gate between the centuries-long time of prophesy, which had closed, and

109 *Qur'án*, Surah 79: 6, 13.
110 *Qur'án*, Surah 2: 206.
111 Nabil, *The Dawnbreakers*, pp. 316.

the time of fulfillment that was beginning with the coming of the Promised One "Baha'u'llah."

> To Israel [the Jewish Faith] He was neither more nor less than the incarnation of the "Everlasting Father", the "Lord of Hosts" come down "with ten thousands of saints"; to Christendom Christ returned "in the glory of the Father," to Shí'ah Islam the return of the Imám Husayn; to Sunní Islam the descent of the "Spirit of God" [Jesus Christ]; to the Zoroastrians the promised Sháh-Bahrám; to the Hindus the reincarnation of Krishna; to the Buddhists the fifth Buddha.[112]

The Promised One of all these Revelations may have come, as promised by Jesus, with a new name, Bahá'u'lláh, which means "The Glory of God." Each individual has a personal right and responsibility to investigate Bahá'u'lláh's revelation and evaluate its validity. Is there a need for new guidance for our times? If so, the greatest proof of a revelation from God is the Holy Scriptures brought by His Messenger. The Scriptures revealed by Bahá'u'lláh proclaim...

> Verily I say, this is the Day in which mankind can behold the Face, and hear the Voice, of the Promised One. The Call of God hath been raised, and the light of His countenance hath been lifted up upon men. It behoveth every man to blot out the trace of every idle word from the tablet of his heart, and to gaze, with an open and unbiased mind, on the signs of His Revelation, the proofs of His Mission, and the tokens of His glory. Great indeed is this Day! ... God grant that the light of unity may envelop the whole earth... This is the changeless Faith of God, eternal in the past, eternal in the future.[113]

---

112 Shoghi Effendi, *God Passes By*, p. 94.

113 Bahá'u'lláh, *Gleanings from the Writings of Bahá'u'lláh*, VII, pp. 10-11; LXX, p, 136.

Unfortunately, believers of past Revelations often have great difficulty accepting that a new Messenger has come. Consider the rejection of Jesus by the Jewish Pharisees; the rejection of Muhammad by the tribal leaders of his time; the rejection of both the Báb and Bahá'u'lláh by the religious leaders of both Shi'a and Sunni Islam.

To maintain that any of the Messengers of God was the last one to appear and that no more Divine Educators will even be sent as the need arises is not logical. It does not follow the guidance or fulfill the promises made to humanity in all the Holy Scriptures.

Just as an individual grows and requires more and more guidance at each stage of life, so also humanity requires more and more guidance at each stage of its development. As promised in all revelations from God, new Messengers will continue to bring that new guidance.

> The Prophets of God should be regarded as physicians whose task is to foster the well-being of the world and its peoples, that, through the spirit of oneness, they may heal the sickness of a divided humanity. ... Little wonder, then, if the treatment prescribed by the physician in this day should not be found to be identical with that which he prescribed before. How could it be otherwise when the ills affecting the sufferer necessitate at every stage of his sickness a special remedy? In like manner, every time the Prophets of God have illumined the world with the resplendent radiance of the Day Star of Divine knowledge, they have invariably summoned its peoples to embrace the light of God through such means as best befitted the exigencies of the age in which they appeared.[114]

---

114 Bahá'u'lláh, *Gleanings from the Writings of Bahá'u'lláh*, XXXIV, p. 80.

> And this is clear: a power above and beyond the powers of nature must needs be brought to bear, to change this black darkness into light, and these hatreds and resentments, grudges and spites, these endless wrangles and wars, into fellowship and love amongst all the peoples of the earth. This power is none other than the breathings of the Holy Spirit and the mighty inflow of the Word of God.[115]

The first quarter of the twenty-first century has seen an unprecedented overload of information. It is crucial to be able to discern truth from falsehood, especially about spiritual matters. The only reliable tool we have for a continuous search for the truth is reason. At this stage of humanity's history, is it rational or reasonable to believe that one person or one group knows God more than another, or is more blessed, or "chosen"? Really? Such misplaced egocentricity seems to be ingrained in human nature and embedded in tribalism. Perhaps this is why we constantly evaluate ourselves to see where we fit within our society. We are constantly recalculating how much better we are than other individuals or groups. We would do well to consider this advice:

> In this day no regard is paid to loftiness or lowliness, to poverty or wealth, to nobility and lineage, to weakness or might. Whosoever recognizeth the incomparable Beloved is the possessor of true wealth, and occupieth a divine station.[116]

How many wars have been fought because of misunderstandings or misinterpretations by leaders in whom we placed our complete trust even though they may have had limited understanding and their decisions may have been tainted by a desire for personal gain or

---

115 'Abdu'l-Bahá, *Selections from the Writings of 'Abdu'l-Bahá*, No. 23, p. 53
116 Bahá'u'lláh, *The Compilation of Compilations*, "Women," No. 2097, p. 359

grandeur. A lack of true knowledge has led to the death of millions in the past and continues to afflict humanity throughout the world. The lack of rational thinking compounded by the lack of true information has led humanity to suffer great failures and misfortunes. Great civilizations have fallen because one group considered themselves superior and thus beyond reproach. All wars have been caused by such irrational thinking. Knowledge perceived and understood by rational souls is spiritual balm offered to us by God when examined fairly.

> In truth, knowledge is a veritable treasure for man, and a source of glory, of bounty, of joy, of exaltation, of cheer and gladness unto him. Happy the man that cleaveth unto it, and woe betide the heedless.[117]

The religion of God is one religion, but it must ever be renewed. Moses, for example, established a Law revealed by God, and through that Mosaic Law the children of Israel were delivered from their ignorance and came into the light. Still, as the years wore on, the radiance of their "religion" passed by, and that bright day turned to night until the star of the Messiah dawned, bringing a course correction and a fuller understanding of God's truth.

> Our meaning is this: the religion of God is one, and it is the educator of humankind, but still, it needs must be made new. When thou dost plant a tree, its height increaseth day by day. It putteth forth blossoms and leaves and luscious fruits. But after a long time, it doth grow old, yielding no fruitage any more. Then doth the Husbandman of Truth take up the seed from that same tree, and plant it in a pure soil; and lo, there standeth the first tree, even as it was before... Note thou carefully that in this world of being, all things must ever be

---

117 Bahá'u'lláh, *Epistle to the Son of the Wolf*, p. 27.

> made new. Look at the material world about thee, see how it hath now been renewed. The thoughts have changed, the ways of life have been revised, the sciences and arts show a new vigor, discoveries and inventions are new, perceptions are new. How then could such a vital power as religion—the guarantor of mankind's great advances, the very means of attaining everlasting life, the fosterer of infinite excellence, the light of both worlds—not be made new? This would be incompatible with the grace and loving-kindness of the Lord...[118]

History shows that the teachings of God's religion can easily become overshadowed by later additions of rituals and practices. Leaders of religion may have added rituals to maintain their power and influence over the believers. Believers may have added other customs and traditions because of their great love for their religion. But these additions resulted from human imagination, not from the Holy Scriptures revealed by the Divine Educators. Probably no one could have imagined that over time these man-made rituals and traditions would greatly obscure the light of their faith. Eventually, a renewal of religion always becomes necessary, and only a new Divine Educator can breathe new life into it.

> In truth, religion is a radiant light and an impregnable stronghold for the protection and welfare of the peoples of the world, for the fear of God impelleth man to hold fast to that which is good, and shun all evil. Should the lamp of religion be obscured, chaos and confusion will ensue, and the light of fairness and justice, of tranquility and peace cease to shine. Unto this will bear witness every man of true understanding.[119]

---

118 'Abdu'l-Bahá, *Selections from the Writings of 'Abdu'l-Bahá*. #23, pp. 51-53.
119 Bahá'u'lláh, *Tablets of Bahá'u'lláh*, p. 125

Based on the above discourse, one can conclude that religion as we know it was not made by God or Divine Educators, but by men to segregate themselves from others.

Twin Stations of the Messengers of God

The Messengers of God have two stations or realities. First is their human station, the physical reality that they share with the rest of humanity. As Manifestations of God in human form, they have the same material needs as other humans and face similar challenges throughout their lives in this world.

The second station, however, is spiritual or divine. The known history of each Manifestation of God shows remarkable similarities. As children, they stood out from other children and even adults by exhibiting what appeared to be innate or God-given knowledge and wisdom, particularly an understanding of spiritual truths. They demonstrated great attachment to God, prayer and service to humanity. Eventually, in various ways they became aware that God had chosen them to serve as His Messenger to this world. Because of their claims to be Messengers of God, all of them were persecuted during their lifetimes, particularly by the clergy. All accepted suffering with radiance and demonstrated the truth of their teachings in their own lives. Some have been living martyrs for their faith while others have given their lives as a sacrifice. All have revealed the Word of God, which became the Holy Scripture for their time.

Like teachers in a school, all these Messengers, these Divine Educators, have full knowledge of the one Religion of God but only teach as much as their students can comprehend. The different revelations, then—which so many people think of as different religions—can be thought of as grades in school. The knowledge acquired in each grade is not made obsolete or contradicted by the lessons of the next grade, but rather is expanded upon so that even greater knowledge and insights can be gained progressively as the student's capacity for understanding grows.

According to the Bahá'í Faith, the latest Divine Educator refers to Himself in the following manner, which further proves the concept that all the Manifestations of God bring to humanity the same concepts but progressively at a higher level of understanding:

> O Jews! If ye be intent on crucifying once again Jesus, the Spirit of God, put Me to death, for He hath once more, in My person, been made manifest unto you... Followers of the Gospel! If ye cherish the desire to slay Muhammad, the Apostle of God, seize Me and put an end to My life, for I am He, and My Self is His Self...[120]

Every Divine Educator delivers God's truth to the age in which He appears and helps humanity connect with God.

> ... Whoso recognizeth them hath recognized God. Whoso hearkeneth to their call, hath hearkened to the Voice of God, and whoso testifieth to the truth of their Revelation, hath testified to the Truth of God Himself. Whoso turneth away from them, hath turned away from God, and whoso disbelieveth in them, hath disbelieved in God. Every one of them is the Way of God that connecteth this world with the realms above, and the Standard of His Truth unto everyone in the kingdoms of earth and heaven. They are the Manifestations of God amidst men, the evidences of His Truth, and the signs of His glory.[121]

A Short History of Religion

Histories of the better-known revelations from God show that no Messenger who revealed Holy Scriptures intended to start a new religion—quite the opposite, in fact. The goal of each Messenger was

---

120 Bahá'u'lláh, *Gleanings from the Writings of Baha'u'llah*, pp. 101-102.
121 Bahá'u'lláh, *Gleanings from the Writings of Baha'u'llah*, XXI, pp.49-

to refresh and renew the revelations of the past and encourage people to turn once again to the religion of God for guidance. Eventually, each of these revelations led to the development of a great civilization that enriched the life of humanity for several centuries.

The revelations prior to the Bahá'í Revelation were all preserved orally before being written down. The Holy Scriptures revealed by the following Messengers have survived:

MESSENGER	YEAR	PLACE	REVELATION	HOLY SCRIPTURE
Krishna	before 1,300 BC	India	Hindu	Four Vedas
Moses (He Who was drawn out of water)	1,200 BC	Egypt	Jewish Faith	Torah (First 5 books of Old Testament)
Zoroaster	700-600 BC	Persia	Zoroastrian Faith	Zend-avesta
Gautama Buddha (Enlightened One)	560 BC	India	Buddhist Faith	Tripataka
Jesus Christ (Anointed One)	1-33 AD	Palestine	Christianity	Gospels (First 4 books of The New Testament)
Muhammad (Apostle of God)	570-632 AD	Arabia	Islam	Qur'án
The Báb (The Gate)	1819-1850 AD	Persia	Báb'í Faith	Tablets composed by the Báb
Bahá'u'lláh (Glory of God)	1817-1892 AD	Persia	Bahá'í Faith	Tablets composed by Bahá'u'lláh

Some Holy Scriptures, however, are so old that the original language in which they were revealed is no longer spoken, and only linguists and religious scholars can understand it. Scholars have undertaken the task of translating these to modern languages, but the accuracy of these translations is debatable. Nevertheless, the followers of each revelation typically accept the validity of their own Holy Scriptures.

Recent Christian research has determined that...

...the books that make up the Bible (Old Testament and New Testament) were written by various people over a period of more than 1,000 years, between 1,200 B.C. and the first century A.D. ... From the first through the fourth centuries and beyond, different church leaders and theologians made arguments about which books belonged in the (New Testament), often casting their opponents as heretics... Over time, the books that were deemed authentic and authoritative by the communities who used them were included in the (Bible) and the rest were discarded. Although the bulk of that editing work ended in the late 300s A.D., the debate over which books were theologically legit continued until at least the 16th century when church reformer Martin Luther published his German translation of the Bible...[H]undreds of texts similar to those found in the New Testament and Old Testament ... didn't make it into the (Bible).[122]

Even to this day, Christian churches do not agree on the books included in the Bible. Most Protestant Bibles have 66 books, 39 in the Old Testament and 27 in the New Testament. The Roman Catholic Bible has 73 books including the 7 known as Apocrypha. And the Ethiopian Orthodox Church Bible contains 81 books.[123]

Although it was many years before the history of the life and teachings of Jesus was written down, Christians generally accept the New Testament as an accurate record of His revelation. The most recognized books in the New Testament are the four Gospels of Matthew, Mark, Luke and John, along with Acts of the Apostles, the letters of Paul and the Book of Revelation often attributed to the Apostle John.

Similarly, the Holy Scripture of Islam, the Qur'án, was first revealed orally by Muhammad in the Arabic language and transcribed by some of his followers. About seven years after Muhammad's death

---

122 Roos (2020), p. 2-3.
123 Roos (2020), p. 4.

in 632 AD, passages of his revelation were gathered from all over Arabia. This first version of the Qur'án continued to be revised, particularly when vowels and dots were added to the Arabic text some 150-300 years later, to clarify the meaning and pronunciation of some words.

For centuries, as Muhammad's teachings spread to other countries, it was forbidden to translate the Qur'án from Arabic to other languages for fear that the text would become corrupted or misrepresented. This placed a burden on believers, who had to learn Arabic to read and understand the text for themselves. Many Muslims relied on clergy to read and interpret the Qur'án for them. The first English translation of the Qur'án was not published until a thousand years later in 1649 AD. Since then, many translations into English and other languages have been published.

No revelation was ever written by the hand of a Messenger Himself until the nineteenth century.

Over time, the clergy and believers of each revelation continually separated themselves from previous religious allegiances and considered the revelations of other Messengers as different religions or faiths—the Jewish Faith, Hindu Faith, Buddhist Faith, Zoroastrian Faith, Christianity and Islam. Each of these religious communities then splintered into numerous sects based on rivaling interpretations of their Scriptures. A multitude of denominations branched off from the early Christian church over issues of authority and doctrine; there are now over thirty thousand sects of Christianity. The followers of Muhammad also fragmented after His death; nearly a hundred different branches of Islam exist today.

In the past, each religious community developed its own hierarchy of leaders—monks, rabbis, priests, pastors, mullas—to study and interpret the Holy Scriptures for the believers. This made some sense before writing was invented and afterward, when basic literacy was not taught to most people. Unfortunately, many religious leaders exploited the trust of the illiterate people they served, finding it easy to promote scriptural interpretations that fit their political agendas, a practice which is visited upon the gullible even today. Many used their religious authority to maintain personal power, wealth and status. Contradictory interpretations of Holy Scripture often produced disunity, conflict and even violence within and between religious communities. Millions of believers have been— and still are—tortured, imprisoned or killed if they do not submit to the interpretations of religious authority figures.

> Leaders of religion, in every age, have hindered their people from attaining the shores of eternal salvation, inasmuch as they held the reins of authority in their mighty grasp. Some for the lust of leadership, others through want of knowledge and understanding, have been the cause of the deprivation of the people. By their sanction and authority, every Prophet of God hath drunk from the chalice of sacrifice...[124]

Like teachers in a school, no Divine Educator can be considered superior to another because of what He teaches. A high school mathematics instructor is not superior to an elementary school teacher of basic arithmetic. This is why it is said:

> The fundamental principle enunciated by Bahá'u'lláh ... is that religious truth is not absolute but relative, that Divine Revelation is a continuous and progressive process, that all the great religions of the world are divine in origin, that their basic principles are in complete harmony, that their aims and purposes are one and the same, that their teachings are but facets of one truth, that their functions are complementary, that they differ only in the nonessential aspects of their doctrines, and that their missions represent successive stages in the spiritual evolution of human society...[125]

124 Bahá'u'lláh, *The Kitáb-i-Íqán* (*The Book of Certitude*), p. 15
125 Shoghi Effendi, *The Promised Day Is Come*, p. v.

Chapter 6:
Understanding Holy Scriptures

Parables and Stories

Many of the Holy Scriptures, especially the Gospels of the New Testament, explain spiritual concepts through parables or stories. These stories usually describe activities that were well known to the intended audience such as fishing, gardening, wedding feasts, relationships between fathers and sons—the usual elements of life. In the Gospels, when the disciples asked Jesus to explain why he used parables, he replied:

> Because it is given unto you to know the mysteries of the kingdom of heaven, but to them (non-believers) it is not given. For whosoever hath, to him shall be given, and he shall have more abundance; but whosoever hath not, from him shall be taken away even that he hath.[126]

If we study all the Scriptures, we can see that they addressed the problems of their time rationally but through symbolic language. In this book, we focus mostly on the Western religious teachings

---

126 *Bible*, Matthew 13: 10-13

because more of our readers are familiar with Jewish, Christian, Islamic and Baha'i Scriptures.

In the nineteenth century, the son of the Prophet-Founder of the Baha'i Faith explained in this way why Jesus used parables or stories to explain spiritual concepts:

> Divine things are too deep to be expressed by common words. The heavenly teachings are expressed in parable in order to be understood and preserved for ages to come. When the spiritually minded dive deeply into the ocean of their meaning they bring to the surface the pearls of their inner significance. There is no greater pleasure than to study God's Word with a spiritual mind.[127]

Many Holy Scriptures also use symbols to explain spiritual concepts. For example, in the New Testament, "bread" or "bread of life" often symbolizes Jesus, the Divine Educator for that age, Who reveals the life-giving "Word of God" which, in one view, is very much like the loving teachings a parent would give to a child.

> The bread of God is he which cometh down from heaven, and giveth life unto the world... I am the bread of life: he that cometh to me shall never hunger; and he that believeth on me shall never thirst... I am the living bread which came down from heaven: if any man eat of this bread, he shall live forever...[128]

> Man shall not live by bread alone, but by every word that proceedeth out of the mouth of God.[129]

---

127 'Abdu'l-Baha, *Abdu'l-Baha in London*, p. 79
128 *Bible*, John 6:33, 35, 51
129 *Bible*, Matthew 4: 4

One way of understanding the symbology of the last sentence of the above quotation is that man lives only by the Word of God. Earthly bread is irrelevant in playing a spiritual role in one's life.

In other passages, "light" symbolizes "knowledge," and "darkness" is used to mean "ignorance." Based on this understanding, when Jesus says "I am come a light into the world, that whosoever believeth in me should not abide in darkness,"[130] it could mean that He has brought knowledge into the world so it would not live in ignorance.

Jesus often spoke in symbolic ways about life and death. Consider this New Testament verse:

> I am the resurrection, and the life: he that believeth in me, though he were dead, yet shall he live.[131]

Jesus makes clear that "life" and "death" have meanings that do not refer to this material world ("though he were dead") but of the awakening of man to his own eternal life. If said by a parent to a child, the message of Jesus's words might be a gentle admonition to think of the future and not be too immersed in playing worldly games, for all such games shall come to an end.

Symbolism is used extensively in the Holy Scripture of Islam, the Qur'án. Knowledge of the conditions of life in Arabia during the seventh century greatly aids in understanding these symbols. Because many of the tribes of Arabia had little knowledge of the Old and New Testament Scriptures during that century, Muhammad educated them with stories from those Writings. This is why many of the symbols used by Muhammad were already familiar to Jews and Christians who were among his audience.

It may be that parables and symbols were also a means of testing the spiritual understanding and loyalty of the believers.

---

130 *Bible*, John 12:46
131 *Bible*, John 11: 25

> ...such things as throw consternation into the hearts of all men come to pass only that each soul may be tested ..., that the truth may be known and distinguished from the false.[132]

> If spiritual truths were told directly and simply, it would be easy for everyone to say they believe. Parables and symbols are a way to distinguish the true from the false, the faithful from the insincere, much as Christ said a shepherd divides his sheep from the goats.[133]

Literal Interpretation Versus Lateral Thinking

Some people find the Scriptures confusing or irrational, and so they turn to their religious leaders for interpretation. This is understandable. Some passages of the Holy Scriptures may seem outdated or too fantastic to believe. This is particularly true when the Writings are interpreted only in literal or material ways. But what if these passages were meant as metaphors for spiritual truths? It may be challenging to consider a different view than the popular belief of the majority. But could it be that the insistence on blind faith in a literal interpretation of certain passages in the Holy Writings is a method of maintaining fear and control over the membership of a group?

In the world of literature, a popular genre of fiction called "magical realism" has been captivating readers since its origins in folklore. Literary scholars trace its antecedents back to the Catholic religion, which fosters a belief in miracles and other spontaneous and ineffable phenomena. In a magical realism novel, fantastical things are treated not just as possible but as real.

In the famous novel *One Hundred Years of Solitude* by Columbian author Gabriel Garcia Marquez, which tells a story that takes place

---

132 Bahá'u'lláh, *The Kitáb-i-Íqán (The Book of Certitude)*, p. 52
133 *Bible*, Mathew 25: 32

over many generations, fantastical things are always happening. A woman, for example, is sucked up to heaven in her own personal rapture; another woman, visited by Death, is told that when she finishes making the shawl that currently occupies her, she will die; in yet another passage, ants devour an infant. These events, though fantastical, are treated just as matter-of-factly as the everyday events in the story.

Unlike fantasy stories, which live in a world of their own, magical realism novels take place in a natural setting familiar to the reader but suggest that the real world has an undercurrent of magic. The fantastical elements are accepted as normal. Like fairy tales and folklore, magical realism blurs the line between fantasy and reality, suggesting that we perhaps live simultaneously in multiple worlds of consciousness or being.

Ordinarily, while enjoying this rich stew of magic and realism, most readers understand that the magical parts are just that—fantasy. Reading these works requires "lateral" thinking—searching for the implied meaning of the story rather than simply taking it literally. Few readers, though willing to suspend belief in magic for the duration of their reading experience, truly believe that the fantastical elements represent reality. But magical realism can be subversive and slowly persuade the reader that the fantastical "could be" or "might be" real after all. The British critic Christopher Warnes defined magical realism as "a mode of narration that naturalizes or normalizes the supernatural." In other words, magical realism can be persuasive by making fantastical events or creatures more accessible.

The elements of magical realism can be found in the sacred Scriptures of all the world's great wisdom traditions from Hinduism to Christianity and beyond. Oddly, the literature that forms the basis for each of these religions is often read by devout believers with total suspension of belief often caused by years of religious education promoting a literal interpretation of the texts. Magical realism, as we call it today, fills the Bible's pages with stories of men who lived nearly a thousand years; races of giants called the Nephilim; sexual unions between angels and humans; unicorns and a dragon-like creature called a Leviathan; a man who survived three days in the belly of a "great fish" (Jonah); and much more. To a fisherman of that time, being "in the belly of a fish" only implied that the man was in great trouble.

The book of Genesis in the Bible's Old Testament has for thousands of years been a mirror or lamp that reveals the nature of human existence, the cosmos and God. The complex inner meanings of the text, however, often get lost in profitless arguments about whether the work should be taken literally or symbolically, whether it is unassailable natural history or an imaginative parable with layers of meaning.

Perhaps this attempt to contrast fiction versus non-fiction draws an illusory line. We prefer to think of Genesis as a work of magical realism that requires the modern mind to read it—as well as all other religious Holy Texts—with a rational mind informed by science, motivated by a search for truth and guided by enlightened teachers who have lit the path to greater knowledge.

The Resurrection Story

Judging from the controversy surrounding them, the creation story of Genesis is perhaps exceeded only by the resurrection story of the Gospels. The purpose of Christ's sacrifice and steadfastness to the Teaching was to ensure that mankind would change its perspective and realize the existence of the next world and the judgments of our reality after death, which are based on reward and punishment.

Is the story of Jesus's resurrection a physical reality or does it refer to a spiritual reality that has been obscured by the insistence of many theologians that it be understood literally? The theme of resurrection is frequently used in the Bible to demonstrate the power of God. In the Old Testament, there are three incidents of physical resurrection after the apparent death of an individual.

1. Elijah asked the Lord to revive the dead son of a widow (1 Kings 17:17–24).
2. Elisha revived a dead child (2 Kings 4: 32–37).
3. A dead man revived when his body touched the bones of Elisha (2 Kings 13: 20–21).

The New Testament records at least six incidents of physical resurrection during the time of Jesus and His disciples.

1. Jesus held the hand of the dead daughter of a ruler, and she revived (Matthew 9:18-19, 23–25).
2. Jesus's command revived the only son of a widow (Luke 7: 12–17).
3. Jesus revived Lazarus four days after his death (John 11: 1-44).
4. Just after Christ's crucifixion, the graves of many saints were opened and many bodies of the saints that "slept" arose (Matthew 27: 52–53).
5. Peter revived Tabitha (Dorcas) at Joppa (Acts 9: 36–41).
6. Paul revived Eutychus after dying from a fall from a third-story window (Acts 20: 9-12).

The most significant example of resurrection for Christians, however, is the belief in the physical resurrection of Jesus after His death by crucifixion. Prophecies about Jesus's death by crucifixion had been revealed in the Psalms of David some one thousand years earlier, but crucifixion was not practiced in Palestine until the time of the Romans. The physical resurrection of Jesus is cited by Christian clergy as a fundamental proof of the Divinity of Jesus, though it is never cited as proof of the Divinity of others in the Bible who were also resurrected.

As Jesus was hanging on the cross, He recalled David's prophecies by reciting the opening line of Psalm 22: "My God, my God, why hast Thou forsaken me?" The Psalms were so well known to the Jewish people that a rabbi (teacher) could simply recite the first line and the believers could recall from memory the rest of the Psalm, which the rabbi would then interpret. By reciting this line, then, Jesus most likely was reminding His followers of later verses in this Psalm that describe the death He was now suffering.

> I am poured out like water, and all my bones are out of joint; my heart is like wax, it is melted within my breast; my strength is dried up like a potsherd, and my tongue cleaves to my jaws; thou dost lay me in the dust of death. Yea, dogs are round about me; a company of evil-doers encircle me; they have pierced my hands and feet – I can count all my bones – they start and gloat over me; they divide my garments among them, and for my raiment they cast lots.[134]

Two criminals were crucified by the Romans either side of Jesus that day as were many others during the rebellion of Barabas. Only Jesus, however, is said to have been resurrected or brought back to life. The other resurrections mentioned in the Bible appear to have been temporary since these people presumably died a second time.

Is it possible that the meaning of Jesus's resurrection was a spiritual concept, not the physical revival of the body? Why is such great importance given to the physical resurrection of Jesus? After all, many people before and since Jesus have come back to life after they were declared dead. What happened to the others whom the Bible records as dying but were then resurrected? Did they go where Christ went after He was resurrected? The purpose of these questions is not to argue the validity of Jesus's resurrection but to explore a rational explanation for the concept of resurrection.

---

134 *Bible*, Psalms 22: 14–18

Jesus said that He is the Light of the World (John 8:12, 9:15). This physical world is limited by time in a continually changing cycle of birth and death. Is it possible to understand Jesus's station and also His resurrection as a spiritual concept?

The recounting of Jesus's death in the Gospels states that for three days His closest disciples suffered grief and confusion at His loss. Could it be said that their faith in the Word of God revealed by Christ was forgotten or "dead" for three days until Mary Magdalene revived or resurrected their faith? Mary reminded the disciples that Jesus's reality was His Words, and those Words did not die and will never die. This indeed was a true and lasting resurrection. Such a rational explanation can give understanding and comfort to people for centuries.

> The resurrections of the [Divine Educators] are not of the body. All Their states, Their conditions, Their acts, the things They have established, Their teachings, Their expressions, Their parables and Their instructions have a spiritual and divine signification, and have no connection with material things. For example, there is the subject of Christ's coming from heaven: it is clearly stated in many places in the Gospel that the Son of man came from heaven, He is in heaven, and He will go to heaven. So in chapter 6, verse 38, of the Gospel of John it is written: "For I came down from heaven"; and also in verse 42 we find: "And they said, Is not this Jesus, the son of Joseph, whose father and mother we know? How is it then that he saith, I came down from heaven?" Also in John, chapter 3, verse 13: "And no man hath ascended up to heaven, but He that came down from heaven, even the Son of man which is in heaven.[135]

---

135 'Abdu'l-Bahá, *Some Answered Questions,*

Observe that it is said, "The Son of man is in heaven," while at that time Christ was on earth. Notice also that it is said that Christ came from heaven, though He came from the womb of Mary, and His body was born of Mary. It is clear, then, that when it is said that the Son of man is come from heaven, this has not an outward but an inward signification; it is a spiritual, not a material, fact. The meaning is that though, apparently, Christ was born from the womb of Mary, in reality He came from heaven, from the center of the Sun of Reality, from the Divine World, and the Spiritual Kingdom. And as it has become evident that Christ came from the spiritual heaven of the Divine Kingdom, therefore, His disappearance under the earth for three days has an inner signification and is not an outward fact. In the same way, His resurrection from the interior of the earth is also symbolical; it is a spiritual and divine fact, and not material; and likewise His ascension to heaven is a spiritual and not material ascension.... In other words, the Cause of Christ was like a lifeless body until the life and the bounty of the Holy Spirit surrounded it. Such is the meaning of the resurrection of Christ, and this was a true resurrection. ...when the truth of this subject becomes clear, and the symbol is explained, science in no way contradicts it; but on the contrary, science and the intelligence confirm it.[136]

How often have we heard the saying "Spare the rod and spoil the child?" Misunderstanding of this axiom derives from the Old Testament verse "Whoever spares the rod hates their children, but the one who loves their children is careful to discipline them."[137] This axiom has often been used to condone the physical beating of

---

136 'Abdu'l-Bahá, *Some Answered Questions*, pp. 103-105.
137 *Holy Bible*, Proverbs 13:24

children as a discipline for disobedience. Yet the rod in the biblical example was the shepherd's rod used to guide a flock of sheep and never to beat them, which would bruise the meat.

The common Old Testament verse "…it is easier for a camel to go through the eye of a needle than for a rich man to enter the kingdom of God," is also one of the most often misunderstood statements. Knowing that the gates of Jerusalem were constructed to be small for defensive purposes, camels had to shed their burdens before entering and being refitted with cargo. These entrance gates were called "eyes of a needle." The meaning of the biblical verse, then, is not that it is impossible for a rich man to enter the kingdom of God but that it is more difficult because one who has many possessions must shed attachment to them before entering.

Reason argues for a symbolic interpretation of these biblical stories, which in no way detracts from the station or mission of Jesus or any other Divine Educator. Those who are attracted to the traditional literal interpretations will undoubtedly continue to view these stories, and many others, as historical documents. But even these individuals may find even greater spiritual meaning in their symbolic value.

Validity of the Divine Educators

Over the centuries, certain individuals have claimed to reveal the Word of God, but many of them spoke falsely. How can one know if someone proclaiming to be a Divine Educator or a "Manifestation of God" is speaking the truth or is a "false prophet?" How can a believer in God independently investigate the validity of a Divine Educator?

A good place to begin such an investigation is by looking into the Holy Scriptures. For example, the Old Testament Prophets give very specific guidance on how and from where the next Prophet or Messenger will come. In addition, Jesus speaks of ways to assess the authenticity of a Divine Educator:

> Beware of false prophets, which come to you in sheep's clothing, but inwardly they are ravening wolves. Ye shall know them by their fruits. Do men gather grapes of thorns, or figs of thistles? Even so every good tree bringeth forth good fruit; but a corrupt tree bringeth forth evil fruit. A good tree cannot bring forth evil fruit, neither can a corrupt tree bring forth good fruit. Every tree that bringeth not forth good fruit is hewn down, and cast into the fire. Wherefore by their fruits ye shall know them.[138]

This analogy teaches us that the fruits of each Divine Educator are the personal example that He set for us and the Holy Scriptures that He delivered. The validity of each Divine Educator can be judged by the guidance contained in these Holy Scriptures. This new guidance is far more important than the physical life of the Messenger or any miracles that may have been performed at that time. False prophets or messengers sometimes may seem to bring good teachings—outwardly, they are dressed in "sheep's clothing"—but their inner reality and motives are self-centered like a "ravening wolf." In contrast, a true Divine Educator lives the life that They prescribe for others. They "practice what they preach." Their words and deeds are a living testimony to the truth of the revelation They bring from God.

> The proof of the validity of a Manifestation of God is the penetration and potency of His Word, the cultivation of heavenly attributes in the hearts and lives of His followers and the bestowal of divine education upon the world of humanity. This is absolute proof. The world is a school in which there must be Teachers of the Word of God. The evidence of the ability of these Teachers is efficient education of the graduating classes.[139]

---

138 *Bible*, Mathew 7: 15-20
139 'Abdu'l-Bahá, *The Promulgation of Universal Peace*, p. 341

Humanity's Rejection of the Word of God

Despite the counsel and warnings of the previous Divine Educator, history repeats itself every time a new Revelation is proclaimed by one of God's chosen Messengers. Inevitably, the clergy and followers of previous Revelations reject the new Divine Educator and His guidance without any investigation of its truth. Muhammad warns against a knee-jerk and untested rejection of a new claimant in these words:

> If an uneducated and foolish man comes to you in that day and speaks of the coming of a new teacher, seek and evaluate his claim. Do not, out of ignorance, reject and bring hurt and destruction to the Divine Educator... Is it not true that every time a divine messenger comes contrary to your ways, you consider yourself proud and go against him?... Woe to those that on that day see truth as lies and get engulfed with their own vain imaginings.[140]

The practice of ignoring Muhammad's advice continues into the present as many religious leaders openly discourage such independent investigation. They have sought to control the minds and souls of believers by asserting the supremacy of their personal divine inspiration and authority. They have tried to secure the unquestioning loyalty of believers with promises of individual salvation and fear of God's wrath for any wrongdoings. The Quran spoke to this when the people of Yathrib became bold and arrogant to Muhammad:

> The example of those who were entrusted with observing the Torah but failed to do so, is that of a donkey carrying books. How evil is the example of those who reject Allah's signs! For Allah does not guide the wrongdoing people.[141]

---

140 *Qur'án*, Surah 15:6, 2:87, 52:11-12
141 *Al-Jumu'ah* 62-5

When people are repressed through blind faith and their vain imaginings give rise to the terror of damnation, harmful religious practices can harden into intractable "traditions." These practices can debase the status of women, often considered the weaker sex, by allowing male domination through forced labor and slavery of women, sexual exploitation and trafficking of females, the horror of child brides, arranged marriages, even the denial of education for girls and women.

In some cases, religious traditions and customs have been tacked onto the Holy Scriptures with the intention of showing the revisionist's love for their faith. Over time, however, these man-made embellishments have often corrupted the true meaning of the Word of God and caused disunity among the believers. Ultimately, the disunity caused by competing interpretations of doctrine and religious practices causes the once-unified body of believers to fracture into separate branches or denominations of the faith community.

> ...the followers of the divine religions have turned away from the principles and ordinances which are essential and unchanging in the Word of God, forsaking those fundamental realities which have to do with the life of the human world, the eternal life—such as the love of God, faith in God, philanthropy, knowledge, spiritual perception, divine guidance–holding these to be contingent and nonessential while wrangling and disagreeing over such questions as whether divorce is lawful or unlawful, or whether this or that observance of a minor law is orthodox and true. The Jews consider divorce lawful; the Catholic Christians deem it unlawful; the outcome is discord and hostility between them. If they would investigate the one fundamental reality underlying the laws revealed by Moses and Christ, this condition of hatred and misunderstanding would be dispelled and divine unity prevail.[142]

---

142 'Abdu'l-Bahá, *The Promulgation of Universal Peace*, p. 445.

The law of Kosher (meaning "clean") is another example of a Judaic law that changed with the advent of Christianity.

> Now, the question of the excellence or baseness of things is determined either by reason or by religious law. Some believe that it is based on religious law: Such is the case with the Jews, who believe that all the commandments of the Torah are binding and that they are matters of religious law rather than of reason. Thus they say that one of the commandments of the Torah is that meat and butter cannot be eaten together, for this is "trefah" (and "trefah" in Hebrew means unclean, while "kosher" means clean). This they say is a question of religious law and not of reason.[143]

A likely reason for kosher laws in the years before Jesus was that most pots and serving dishes were made of clay, which was porous and difficult to clean after eating meat-based food and before consuming dairy-based food. Failure to thoroughly clean the meat from the dishes sometimes caused disease. For this reason, a law was introduced requiring households to keep two sets of eating dishes—one for meat-based foods and another for dairy products. Today, the Kosher certificate for food manufacturers is a big business with its own label. By the time of Jesus, the process of glazing pottery had been invented, and so keeping separate dishes for meat and dairy became unnecessary. So Jesus abolished that particular law.

The discouragement of individual freedom of thought in matters of conscience and belief can lead believers to blind faith, superstition and fanaticism. Of course, attempts to remove religion from the life of society can be equally destructive, leading to a decline in social and moral standards.

---

143 'Abdu'l-Bahá, *Some Answered Questions*, p. 267.

> Religion is verily the chief instrument for the establishment of order in the world and of tranquility amongst its peoples. The weakening of the pillars of religion hath strengthened the foolish and emboldened them and made them more arrogant... The greater the decline of religion, the more grievous the waywardness of the ungodly. This cannot but lead in the end to chaos and confusion.[144]

Every Divine Educator has suffered and made great sacrifices—some have even given their lives—as they were teaching the Word of God. All the Holy Scriptures deliver a message of the need for love and unity, so why is it that the leadership and the believers of each religious community have all strayed so far from the original Teachings that were given to them? Do the traditions and practices of a religious community promote love and unity, or are they a cause of disunity and separation? Are the community's precious traditions and practices based on the Holy Scriptures or simply man-made additions? Many say that Sunday in the West is the most divisive day of the week because so many people are segregating themselves in their churches to contemplate how much better and more correct they are than those in other churches.

Is it time for a renewal of religion based on rational teachings appropriate to our time?

Consider the following passages and ask yourself if they would promote love and unity and if they are reasonable and logical for our time.

> So powerful is the light of unity that it can illuminate the whole earth.[145]

---

144 Bahá'u'lláh, *Tablets of Bahá'u'lláh*, pp. 63-64.
145 Bahá'u'lláh, *Gleanings from the Writings of Bahá'u'lláh*, CXXXII, p. 288.

Consort with all religions with amity and concord, that they may inhale from you the sweet fragrance of God.[146]

Regard man as a mine rich in gems of inestimable value. Education can, alone, cause it to reveal its treasures and enable mankind to benefit therefrom.[147]

One of the potentialities hidden in the realm of humanity was the capability or capacity of womanhood. Through the effulgent rays of divine illumination the capacity of woman has become so awakened and manifest in this age that equality of man and woman is an established fact...[148]

In the Bahá'í view, recognition of the oneness of mankind "calls for no less than the reconstruction and the demilitarization of the whole civilized world—a world organically unified in all the essential aspects of its life, its political machinery, its spiritual aspiration, its trade and finance, its script and language, and yet infinite in the diversity of the national characteristics of its federated units."[149]

---

146 Bahá'u'lláh, *Tablets of Bahá'u'lláh*, p. 22

147 Bahá'u'lláh, *Tablets of Bahá'u'lláh*, p. 162.

148 *Women*, Compiled by the Research Department of the Universal House of Justice, p. 9

149 "The Promise of World Peace," A letter to the generality of humankind from the Universal House of Justice, p. 13

Chapter 7:
The Education Imperative

Education Defined

When we gaze at the night sky or study the minute particles of an atom, it is clear that knowledge is nearly infinite. When we consider the wonders of the human body, we realize that there are so many unanswered questions that we will never be capable of knowing everything. However, as knowledge is acquired and our understanding matures, we can feel confident that more mysteries of the universe will be discovered.

> **Man is the supreme Talisman. Lack of a proper education hath, however, deprived him of that which he doth inherently possess. Regard man as a mine rich in gems of inestimable value. Education can, alone, cause it to reveal its treasures, and enable mankind to benefit therefrom...**[150]

Education is a basic human right often unacknowledged or denied. It empowers every individual to search for truth and acquire information and knowledge of both the seen and unseen. Education

---

150 Bahá'u'lláh, *Gleanings from the Writings of Bahá'u'lláh*, Section 122, p. 259-260.

is the best means to overcome the inequities and injustices in the world today. With better education for everyone, new ways will be created to promote unity, justice and the well-being of humanity.

Education is the first logical step toward establishing justice. Universal education—educating everyone to read and write and think for themselves—is a fundamental requirement for empowering justice. Consider the injustice of the extremes of wealth. Most poverty, at least in the so-called first world, is exacerbated by a lack of education, which should supply the knowledge and skills required for us to progress materially and provide a stable future for ourselves and our families. The knowledge gained enables individuals to benefit from existing laws and benefits provided by social, civil and political systems to lift them out of poverty.

The word "education" comes from the Latin word *educatus* meaning to rear, to bring up, to provide training or schooling. In ancient Rome, education originally referred to the training of the body, but over time its meaning came to include training of the mind as well. Physical training focused on developing strength and special skills for athletics and battle, whereas education of the mind explored a philosophical evaluation of life.

Similar distinctions in education continue to this day. Some branches of education focus on training for technical vocations that provide society with workers such as carpenters, plumbers, mechanics and electricians. Other vocations require extensive academic study. These include accountants, architects, doctors, engineers, lawyers, teachers— all the professions and intellectual seats of influence. All vocations provide vital services in today's increasingly complex global society. Life experience will always be important in the job market, but also having a certificate in a technical field seems to ensure a better income.

The first systematic efforts to train the mind and explore the meaning of life originated with the world's Holy Scriptures. The first teachers of humanity were the Divine Educators who delivered these Writings. For centuries, humanity has learned important lessons from these recorded texts as well as the interpretations of these Writings and the personal ideas of many religious leaders.

It is no accident that the first schools that focused on the education of the mind, or "rational soul," were organized by religious communities. Early on, the Jewish community introduced religious training for young boys. Completing the curriculum culminated in each youth's *bar mitzvah* during which he would be required to recite verses from the Torah in the original Hebrew language.

In many Christian traditions, youths were required to go through a period of spiritual training before becoming confirmed members of their church. Some went on to become priests or pastors after further study in monasteries or seminaries. In the earliest centuries of the faith of Muhammad, the spiritual training of youth occurred in special schools called *madrassahs* where youth learned to read and write the Qur'án in the original Arabic language. By the end of the eleventh century AD, a network of madrassahs had grown throughout the region from Mesopotamia to northeastern Persia.

The Objective of Education

A primary objective of education is not to lay down laws and ordinances but to develop the talents and capacities of each individual.

> Regard man as a mine rich in gems of inestimable value. Education can, alone, cause it to reveal its treasures, and enable mankind to benefit therefrom.[151]

> The possessors of sciences and arts have a great right among the people of the world. Indeed, the real treasury of man is his knowledge. Knowledge is the means of honor, prosperity, joy, gladness, happiness and exaltation.[152]

---

151 Bahá'u'lláh, *Tablets of Bahá'u'lláh*, p. 162.
152 Bahá'u'lláh, *Tablet of Tajallíyát*.

It seems reasonable that individuals should be trained and motivated to devote their lives to service for the well-being and progress of humanity. How unfortunate would it be, then, if religious leaders misused training to control and dominate their followers through indoctrination or brainwashing? How regrettable as well if schools were to neglect character development and focus only on skills to acquire material wealth and financial success at the expense of spiritual understanding and growth. Yet this is often the case.

When the full capacity of education is fully and justly applied, it can accomplish much more than the simple transfer of knowledge from one generation to the next. But this can only occur if good teachers strive to train the next generation to study and search for truth independently, not based on any prejudices or the preconceived ideas of others.

Even the Divine Educators—the Messengers of God—have declared that They are merely channels through which the Word of God flows to humanity through their Teachings. They have made clear that the Holy Writings do not come from Themselves, but from God. These Messengers have also made clear that, if given the choice, They would never have accepted the trials and tribulations of Their earthly roles. Nevertheless, They gladly sacrificed Their lives to share the teachings of God with humanity.

Christ prayed to God, for example, to be relieved of His role:

> **And he said, Abba, Father, all things are possible unto thee; take away this cup from me: nevertheless not what I will, but what thou wilt.**[153]

The most recent Divine Educator, referred to in Quran as the "The Ancient Beauty," described His exile and imprisonment at the hands of the religious clergy:

---

153 *Bible*, Mark 14: 36

> The Ancient Beauty hath consented to be bound with chains that mankind may be released from its bondage, and hath accepted to be made a prisoner within this most mighty Stronghold that the whole world may attain unto true liberty. He hath drained to its dregs the cup of sorrow, that all the peoples of the earth may attain unto abiding joy, and be filled with gladness... He Who hath come to build anew the whole world, behold, how they that have joined partners with God have forced Him to dwell within the most desolate of cities![154]

We are told that the foundation of all education in this time must focus on the development of character and an attitude of service based on the Holy Scriptures.

> The source of all learning is the knowledge of God, exalted be His glory, and this cannot be attained save through the knowledge of His Divine Manifestation... Thus, whoso attains to the knowledge of the Manifestations of God attains to the knowledge of God, and whoso remains heedless of Them remains bereft of that knowledge.[155]

In our time, many individuals are either ignorant about the Divine Educators or claim they do not believe in God. Instead, they follow only what they can see and experience in the world of nature. We have been told, however, that in our search for truth, everyone should be open-minded while understanding that this earthly life is very short.

---

154 Bahá'u'lláh, *Gleanings from the Writings of Bahá'u'lláh*, XLV, p. 99-100.
155 'Abdul'Bahá, *Some Answered Questions*, Part 4, Section 59.

> It behoveth everyone to traverse this brief span of life with sincerity and fairness. Should one fail to attain unto the recognition of Him Who is the Eternal Truth, let him at least conduct himself with reason and justice.[156]

In the world today, politics and sports seem to have a greater influence over many people's lives than involvement with a faith community. A common culture or agreement on ideas and beliefs often permeates the atmosphere of political and sporting affiliations. Unfortunately, many of these unifying beliefs derive from long-held prejudices that are expressions of an emotional commitment to ignorance. How can such prejudices be eliminated and the disunity of people be overcome?

Three Kinds of Education

We have explored two kinds of education—that of the body and the mind. And we have considered the need for divine or spiritual education. This third kind of education aims to promote the happiness, well-being, spiritual upliftment and freedom of humanity as summarized in this passage:

> ...education is of three kinds: material, human and spiritual. Material education is concerned with the progress and development of the body, through gaining its sustenance, its material comfort and ease. This education is common to animals and man...
>
> Human education signifies civilization and progress—that is to say, government, administration, charitable works, trades, arts and handicrafts, sciences, great inventions and discoveries and elab-

---

156 Bahá'u'lláh, *The Summons of the Lord of Hosts*, p. 168

> orate institutions, which are the activities essential to man as distinguished from the animal.
>
> Divine education is that of the Kingdom of God: it consists in acquiring divine perfections, and this is true education; for in this state man becomes the focus of divine blessings, the manifestation of the words, "Let Us make man in Our image, and after Our likeness." (Genesis 1:26) This is the goal of the world of humanity.
>
> Now we need an educator who will be at the same time a material, human and spiritual educator, and whose authority will be effective in all conditions.[157]

Humanity needs all three kinds of education. If only the body and mind are trained, it can encourage selfish demands and desires, vanity, pride and attachment to the things of this world. In contrast, divine or spiritual education inspires selflessness, self-sacrifice, humility and detachment from worldly things. Spiritual education also opens our spiritual eyes to the reality of the next world, a condition free from the limitations of this world. A person who has been trained by all three kinds of education can utilize his rational soul to its full extent, living well in this world while anticipating the next.

We all know that we will die someday. But most people avoid thinking and talking about death, focusing instead on their earthly possessions, status in society and their physical and mental well-being. It is difficult to imagine leaving all these things behind, of course, and entering a new and unknown existence after the death of the body.

Fortunately, a spiritual education prepares us for this eventual outcome by strengthening our spiritual qualities. A person who is well-trained in this way regards death as a "messenger of joy" and a

---

157 'Abdu'l-Bahá, *Some Answered Questions*, Part 1, Section 3.

second "birth" into a new existence that brings them ever closer to the knowledge of the Creator. One's spiritual condition in this new existence does not depend on achievements in the material world but is based on the acquisition of everlasting virtues.

Often in this temporal life we see deeply spiritual persons who have limited material wealth but are content and have no fear of death, while other persons who are attached to wealth and status consider suicide preferable to life when disaster strikes or are so unsatisfied with their existence that they take their own lives. We fashion our own "hell" or "heaven" on this earth.

The Importance of Universal Education

A lack of universal education has often led to blind faith in the teachings of political and religious leaders. Blind faith is an absolute acceptance of the ideas proclaimed by these leaders even when those ideas are not rational. Throughout history, many self-seeking leaders fostered ignorance among their followers to reduce resistance by more rational parties and gain absolute authority over everyone. In the case of religious leaders, the original teachings revealed by their Divine Educators were rational and promoted the well-being of humanity, but over time so many man-made practices were introduced that the light of the original teachings gradually became obscured and finally extinguished.

Recall how the people of Jesus's time blindly followed the religious leaders of their era. These self-serving religious leaders clung to their power over the people and refused to accept that a new Revelation had come, as had been foretold in their own Scriptures. Jesus spoke of His impending trial and the tribulations He would suffer, as had also been prophesied. His devoted disciple, Peter, begged him not to go to Jerusalem because the well-known prophecies clearly stated He would be killed there.

Jesus responded that it was the Will of God for Him to come to such an end, therefore no one should try to change His journey there. Jesus was so firm in this conviction and grew so frustrated by

Peter's attempts to keep Him away from Jerusalem that He called His disciple "Satan," a term meaning "breaker of the covenant." Whenever the followers of a Divine Educator are kept ignorant and compelled to blindly follow their leaders, history repeats itself. Slander, cruelty, oppression, persecution, torture and execution soon follow.

Universal education is the only way to prevent such disasters. There must be a clear understanding of religious truth by everyone.

> ...the bedrock of Bahá'í belief (is) the principle that religious truth is not absolute but relative, that Divine Revelation is orderly, continuous and progressive and not spasmodic or final... "To believe that all revelation is ended, that the portals of Divine mercy are closed..." must constitute in the eyes of every follower of the Faith a grave, an inexcusable departure from one of its most cherished and fundamental principles."[158]

The Dark Side of Education

Education, however, has the same perils today as all other forms of communication. Schools, workshops, courses and retreats can all be used to coerce or persuade students to believe the truth as defined by the educator or sponsor. When a charismatic "educator" wearing the mantle of authority speaks, his or her words can influence an audience disproportionately to the truth contained in the message. Cleverly manipulated "facts" can deceive even the brightest minds. We have seen an entire nation educated to believe that it is not only acceptable but preferable to exterminate all Jews.

In many ways, education can be as dangerous as social media when used irresponsibly. The remedy, as always, is personal investigation of truth by fearlessly asking questions, doing hard research, drawing one's own conclusions, challenging authority figures with one's

---

158 Bahá'u'lláh, quoted by Shoghi Effendi in *The World Order of Bahá'u'lláh*, pp. 115-116.

reservations. Red flags—whether the subject is religious, political or academic—are always the same. If you are encouraged or pressured into accepting what is being taught, trust your instincts. If you are discouraged from making inquiries, step up and ask your questions. If a group attempts to apply social pressure to bend your beliefs to the majority, go the other way.

When education promotes concepts that defy reason, it is fair to call those teachings opinions or theories, but certainly not to present them as facts. A classic example of this is the concept of heaven and hell. There is no doubt that the Scriptures of Christianity and Islam refer to these outcomes in vivid language, but there is considerable doubt about whether the presentation of these ideas used memorable metaphors or revealed actual places. Fundamentalists propose that hell is a physical place, and the torments described are to be taken literally.

The concepts of heaven and hell derive from ancient beliefs in a constant conflict between right and wrong, light and darkness, knowledge and ignorance, reward and punishment. Most Jews had no understanding of hell and heaven until the Hebrew prophet Daniel (620–538 BC) returned from Persia where he studied the Zoroastrian religion. Daniel began teaching the concepts he had learned there including life after death, resurrection of the soul and the day of judgement. These concepts, when taught to his fellow Jews, prepared them to understand the message of Jesus. It was the Zoroastrian kings, sometimes called the "Magi of the East," who were the first to recognize the infant Jesus as a Manifestation of God and visited Him in Bethlehem.

Particularly in Christianity and Islam, the concepts of reward and punishment came to be associated with actual places in the next world. The Teachings of Jesus were modified after His death to conform to interpretations that evolved into the concepts of hell, heaven and purgatory.

Many of the images of hell and heaven so familiar today derive not from Holy Scriptures but from a narrative poem, *The Divine*

Comedy, written in the early 1300s by an Italian, Dante Alighieri. This poem's imaginative vision of the next world describes hell as a burning inferno. It introduces the concept of purgatory and depicts heaven as a beautiful garden paradise. The most important painter of the Renaissance, Botticelli (1445–1510), dedicated a decade to painting and drawing hell as Dante had described it. Both Dante's poem and the artwork derived from it were creative works of the imagination inspired by ancient beliefs and visualized literally. The impact of these images helped solidify hell and heaven as indelible physical places and the torments as actual tortures.

For centuries, countless artists have taken inspiration from *The Divine Comedy* to create paintings, sculptures, music and literature, all of which have reinforced belief that the imaginary domains described by Dante are physical realities. Many religious leaders took advantage of the irrational fear caused by these man-made images, and some religious leaders continue to do so.

No one who believes such a myth dares to ask if hell and heaven are real places for fear that their questions will increase the chance they will be assigned to the hotter destination. Even in this age of space exploration, when we can precisely locate millions of celestial bodies, no one who believes hell and heaven are real places questions their physical location. Belief in hell and heaven has been accepted on blind faith for over seven hundred years and is still perpetuated by various religious leaders to maintain control over their believers.

When a lie is repeated often enough by many people, society begins to accept the lie as truth without any proof of its reality. Belief in the lie may linger in society for months or years. We sometimes label people who irrationally accept such lies as extremists, fanatics or fundamentalists.

Through unbiased education and independent investigation, is it reasonable to consider that the concepts of hell and heaven do not describe "places" but are instead metaphors for "conditions of the spirit?" Could hell simply be a way to describe the eventual agony of how turning away from God and His guidance results in distancing oneself from God, whereas heaven perhaps is a heartening way of describing a condition of nearness to God and obedience to His Teachings? Could heaven be compared to being in the light of spiritual guidance and hell the turning away from this light or perhaps making a choice to be in darkness? These are useful definitions of knowledge and ignorance.

Such a rational understanding of hell and heaven can explain how it is possible to experience both hell and heaven while still on Earth as well as after the death of the body. How many times have we heard people say that they were in hell during wars, or that they were in heaven when reunited with loved ones? Such an understanding removes all fear of death and allows each person to become like a bird freed from the prison of its cage to soar into the unimaginable realms of nearness to God.

> The world is but a show, vain and empty, a mere nothing, bearing the semblance of reality. Set not your affections upon it. Break not the bond that uniteth you with your Creator, and be not of those that have erred and strayed from His ways. Verily I say, the world is like the vapor in a desert, which the thirsty dreameth to be water and striveth after it with all his might, until when he cometh unto it, he findeth it to be mere illusion.[159]

---

159 Bahá'u'lláh, *Gleanings from the Writings of Bahá'u'lláh*, CLIII, p. 328.

Chapter 8:
Religious Communities

Are We Rational Beings?

It is important to establish that humans must be rational beings because they can explain everything rationally or reasonably. Yet people often suppress this ability when religious questions are examined. This is understandable because many passages from the Holy Scriptures of the past do not seem rational or logical. It can be easy to make exceptions for Scripture because it is thought of as supernatural or spiritual and not material or rational. Consequently, many rational people simply shift their brains into neutral when reading or thinking about religious teachings. "This doesn't need to be logical" is a common mindset when it comes to religious topics. This, of course, compromises or eliminates rational thinking altogether, eventually leading to a cultural or political system based primarily on emotion and irrational behavior.

Changes in society are occurring quickly in this age of mass communications and massive migrations. Research conducted on new American immigrants[160] revealed that with each generation came a decline in religious affiliation. On arrival, 63 percent of younger

---

160 Pew Research Center, a non-partisan American think tank based in Washington, D.C. 2022.

immigrants between eighteen and twenty-nine years of age and 37 percent of older immigrants in this age group professed an affiliation with a particular religious community. By the third generation in America, however, 70 percent said they had no religious affiliation.

In addition, religious affiliation declined as income increased: 41 percent of immigrants with $30,000 or less income and 86 percent with $100,000 or more income had no religious affiliation. Higher levels of education were also correlated with a significant decline in religious affiliation: about 43 percent of those with no college education declared a specific religious affiliation, but only 39 percent of those with some college education and just 14 percent of college graduates had a religious affiliation.

When immigrants were questioned about their personal beliefs, 21 percent indicated that they absolutely believed in God, while nearly twice as many—about 39 percent—said they did not believe in God. Of these same participants, 9 percent said religion was very important, while 39 percent said religion was not important at all. Only 4 percent of this group attended religious services, while 68 percent seldom or never attended. When it came to how they make personal decisions in life, only 5 percent depended on religion, 19 percent depended on science, and the vast majority—about 53 percent—relied on common sense.

While not definitive, these statistics seem to indicate that a large percentage of young Americans have no religious affiliation and rely more on science and common sense in making decisions for their lives. Other statistics for the years 2018 to 2022 show an increase in the number of people who say religion does not play a role in their lives. From the data, then, it appears most younger people depend on rational thinking to make moral decisions or judgments.

Similar statistics from European countries and Canada indicate that these nations are also experiencing a steady abandonment of religious affiliation. Similar trends seem to be occurring worldwide. From 1981 to 2007, most countries that were studied became increasingly religious. For the next thirteen years, though, up to 2020, an overwhelming number of these countries became less religious. The United States showed the largest decline.

Understanding that the reality of human beings is mainly their thoughts, and rational thinking guides these thoughts in most people, it seems logical that for humanity to advance requires even more people to think and make decisions rationally in every area of life. Becoming a "complete human," then, implies reliance on rational thinking and reasonable behavior.

Is it possible that more people thinking rationally about all things could lead to a new way of life for humanity, even a new way of organizing the world? Logically, the authors suggest, the goal of such a new society would be to promote the unity and lasting peace of all humanity.

> The world of humanity shall become the manifestation of the lights of Divinity, and the bestowals of God shall surround all. From the standpoints of both material and spiritual civilization extraordinary progress and development will be witnessed. In this present cycle there will be an evolution in civilization unparalleled in the history of the world. The world of humanity has, heretofore, been in the stage of infancy; now it is approaching maturity.[161]

Even though humanity is lurching toward this goal, outdated religious and social standards perpetuate barriers to unity and lasting peace. So, why do divisive political practices and religious communities that are hostile to progress continue to exist? Is it only because of our need for social contact or our desire to belong to a special group, or, as has been suggested, are there those among us who have a desire for divinity?

---

161 'Abdu'l-Bahá, *The Promulgation of Universal Peace*, pp. 37-38

Why are more and more people rejecting or discontinuing their affiliation with religious communities? Is it because more and more people are now putting greater reliance on science and rational thinking rather than on blind faith or irrational beliefs? It certainly is not that humans are becoming less social or associating with fewer groups, but less frequently they are joining a religious community.

Our Need to Belong

During a recent discussion, a friend seemed intent on revealing his political affiliation. He began by sharing his experience of telling his sister at a family gathering that he had joined a different political group than the rest of the family. He explained that his relatives, who did not share the convictions of his new political allies, were stunned and spoke out strongly against his decision. The memory of that heated confrontation obviously still bothered him.

His decision to join this group provoked some important questions. Was this friend aware of how other people, including his family, viewed his new political group? Did the members of the group he had joined fully understand the group's policies and goals before joining? Did those policies and goals agree with the cultural backgrounds and experiences of all its members?

All individuals develop a personal understanding of this material world based on their backgrounds, life experiences and beliefs. It would be impossible for a group or organization to perfectly match the beliefs and expectations of every member. So, why are people so determined to belong to a group? It seems that "belonging" is such a basic human need that people join groups even if it means they must ignore some of the details they don't accept.

A Christian once boasted about how wonderful his faith was and how lofty its standards. He was asked to explain the difference between himself and the felons convicted of serious crimes who also claimed to be Christians. His response, a common one, was simply, "Those people are not true Christians." In this case, the remark was made by a Christian but could easily have been made by the follower of any religion. We feel free to judge who is devout and who is not.

Who among us has the authority to determine which person is true to his Faith and which is not? Is a true Christian one who has not been caught committing an act that is unchristian? One way of looking at this issue is to recognize that we are all "becoming" Christians, Jews or Muslims, and no one has yet graduated from their class with special authority to judge others.

In none of the Holy Writings is the right to judge another person's soul granted to an individual. The Scriptures have given humanity the Teachings to follow but do not give man the right to enforce them. One explanation for this is that the Teachings make a covenant between the Teacher and the individual who professes belief in them, and this covenant does not exist for someone who does not promise to follow those Teachings. Therefore, in most cases, punishments for disobedience to the Teachings of Scripture have been prescribed by other followers, not by the Holy Writings.

When asked, many people who profess to be Christians or Jews or Muslims confess that they know very little about the Teachings of their religions. Many have not read their own Scriptures. Nevertheless, they still claim a specific religious affiliation.

Why do we need to classify ourselves as members of a group? Why are we reluctant to clarify what we understand or believe if it's different from the group's beliefs? Are we afraid that our personal views will be rejected? Why can't we simply say who we are and what we believe and not hitch our wagon to a group that may or may not meet many of our standards? Is it possible to say honestly what we believe in such a way that the person we tell does not become upset and defensive?

Since everyone, at least most of whom we might classify as neurotypical, has a unique capacity to think rationally and develop their own understanding, a good way to find common ground with others is to openly discuss a topic using rational or reasonable proofs. Of course, this also requires us to listen respectfully and with an open mind to the logical arguments of others. This often results in both sides reaching a rational conclusion while preserving friendship. Consulting with others in this way encourages us to do some research and thinking before presenting our views. It also nurtures a posture of humility as we wholeheartedly accept that we do not know everything and should be open to learning from others. From the perspective and the words of a Divine Educator:

> "God witnesseth and [all] the atoms of existences testify that we have mentioned that which will be the cause of the exaltation, elevation, education, preservation, and reformation of the dwellers upon earth. We desire of God that He will strengthen [His] servants. That which this Oppressed One seeketh of all is justice and fairness: let them not be satisfied with listening; let them ponder on what hath become manifest from this Oppressed One. I swear by the Sun of Revelation, which hath shone forth from the horizon of the heaven of the Kingdom of the Merciful One, that, if any [other] expositor or speaker had been beheld, I would not have made Myself an object for the malevolence and the calumnies of mankind."[162]

As humanity slowly moves toward the age of maturity, everyone should be actively engaged in discussing issues of importance to our global society based on shared understanding and perceptions. Every discussion can be a learning opportunity for all.

The Influence of Affiliations

An old poem from the East expounds upon the effects of association with a simple story. In those days, people in a public bath would enjoy hours of thorough scrubbing, soaking and massage. One day,

---

162 *A Traveler's Narrative*, p. 85

a man went to the public bath with a pumice stone given to him by a friend. As he began scrubbing his feet and heels with the rough stone, he noticed a wonderful, rose-like fragrance.

He asked the stone, "What are you, a stone or a flower?"

The stone responded, "I was a stone with no fragrance until I began to associate with roses. The very essence of these flowers then penetrated every part of me until I took on their fragrance. Otherwise, as you can see, I am just a coarse stone."

The moral of this ancient story is that the people with whom we are affiliated in various ways have a great influence on our education, knowledge and behavior. Over time, the ideas of those with whom we associate fill our mind until we eventually begin to think and act alike. This simple story explains how our thoughts can easily be influenced by friends and acquaintances when we are not using our rational thinking. The effects can be good or bad just as such information can be true or false. Thinking is not rational unless it is done independently and based on objective search, not influenced by our peers no matter how we may like them. As we socialize with others, we should always be aware that our thoughts can easily be swayed toward their point of view, which may not be valid or reasonable.

> **Wealth maketh many friends; but the poor is separated from his neighbor.**[163]

> **Close friends will be enemies to one another on that Day, except the righteous.**[164]

> **O MY SON! The company of the ungodly increaseth sorrow, whilst fellowship with the righteous cleanseth the rust from off the heart. He that seeketh to com-**

---

163 *Bible*, Proverbs 19: 4.
164 Ḥâ-Mîm, 67

> mune with God, let him betake himself to the companionship of His loved ones; and he that desireth to hearken unto the word of God, let him give ear to the words of His chosen ones.[165]

> O FRIEND! In the garden of thy heart plant naught but the rose of love, and from the nightingale of affection and desire loosen not thy hold. Treasure the companionship of the righteous and eschew all fellowship with the ungodly.[166]

Sound, rational thinking implies that in social settings we take care so that those around us do not infuse their ideas into the information they share. This is particularly true in religious, political and social gatherings.

Consider, for example, the traditions and practices of some major religious communities. The Jewish Scriptures date back some 3,000 years, the Christian Scriptures over 2,000 years and the Qur'an—as well as the traditions or *hadíths* of Islam—more than 1,000 years. How can we be sure that no changes have been made in these Scriptures through subsequent translations and interpretations? Most of the Holy Scriptures of the past were handed down by word of mouth before being transcribed. The early languages in which these Scriptures were recorded either do not exist or have evolved so that the meaning of many words has changed considerably. This does not mean that these Scriptures were not divinely inspired when delivered, but rather that it can be hard to reconcile their original meaning with our interpretation of them today.

In an era of "fake news," it is increasingly difficult to determine the validity of information, even images. Recent technological

---

165 Bahá'u'lláh, *The Hidden Words of Bahá'u'lláh*, from the Persian, Number 56
166 Bahá'u'lláh, *The Hidden Words of Bahá'u'lláh*, from the Persian, Number 3

advances now enable production of "deep fake" videos of a person in which their face or body has been digitally altered so they appear to be someone else. This can be used maliciously to spread false information about or from a seemingly credible source. If we cannot trust what we see or hear, how can we know if the information is true?

Most fake information uses some element of truth as its foundation. When it is believed by someone we associate with, and see as credible, the false message can be passed on to us like a virus. Initially, the false message starts from a point of acceptance or agreement about something that is true, and false or misleading information is gradually added until the recipient becomes totally deceived. The best protection against such manipulation is to engage our rational thinking and innate wisdom to detect the unproven and often misleading parts of a message.

Questions become the tools of choice for rational thought. Who or what is the source of the information and what are they trying to sell? What ideas does the message aim to promote? Critical thinking can help reveal the motivation behind a message, and this often reveals the truth or deception.

God-made Vs. Man-made Teachings

When reflecting on the teachings and practices of a religious community, it seems reasonable to explore which of their teachings are God-made—that is, documented in the Holy Scriptures—and which teachings or practices are later additions by fallible humans. Is it mostly the man-made rules and regulations that have caused so many people to reject affiliation with any religious community? If so, can religious communities ever return to a focus on God-made teachings?

Almost certainly, from the beginning of each religious community, worship of God has been a personal and private matter based on the understanding of oral teachings derived originally from the Divine Messengers. Over time, however, believers started bonding into special gatherings for communal or group worship. How and why did these gatherings become the focus of worship? In Christianity, the concept of "church" was first recorded in the Gospel of Matthew:

> He saith unto them, But whom say ye that I am? And Simon Peter answered and said, Thou art the Christ, the Son of the living God. And Jesus answered and said unto him, Blessed art thou, Simon Barjona: for flesh and blood hath not revealed it unto thee, but my Father which is in heaven. And I say also unto thee, That thou art Peter, and upon this rock I will build my church...[167]

Jesus Christ said that the Father (God) revealed this truth to Simon, indicating that this was a spiritual relationship, not one of flesh and blood. To strengthen this revelation, Jesus gave Simon a new name, Peter, which in Greek means "rock," confirming that this spiritual relationship between God and humanity would be a strong foundation—the rock—on which Christ's church would be built.

In Christianity, the word "church" came to be understood as the "true body of Christians"—those who believed in the close spiritual relationship between God, Jesus and His followers. Roman Catholics refer to the church as all people who have been regenerated by the Holy Spirit.

Protestant Christians in the 1500s interpreted "church" to mean "the Word of God purely preached and listened to, and the sacraments administered according to Christ's institution." This was referred to as the "Church Invisible." The word "church" in all its translations also acquired the meaning of a building in which believers worshiped together led by an individual who was accepted as the representative of Jesus, while Jesus remained the true head of the Church.

---

167 *Bible*, Mathew 16:15-18

There are two problems with these definitions of "church." First, defining "church" as the "true body of Christians" caused many believers to sit in judgment of others to determine who was truly qualified to be included in this esteemed body. To be eligible, one had to be "regenerated" or "born again," the definitions of which vary by sect. Second, defining "church" as a particular building or place tended to strengthen divisions among believers based on variations in their beliefs. Affiliation with a particular church often became a focus of social status rather than a spiritual relationship with God and Jesus.

Could it be that by "church" Jesus meant a spiritual relationship? That the belief of the followers of Jesus is the "church" of Christianity, not the building itself? If so, by "church" Jesus introduced the concept of a deeply personal relationship with God.

It would seem that only through the thoughts and deeds of individuals who follow the teachings of Jesus can the "church" become obvious to others. So, based on this information, it appears that Christianity was a very personal concept of religion from the very beginning. The deeds of an individual identified them as followers of Jesus. Their affiliation with Jesus had nothing to do with a physical building or even a name or title they chose to give themselves.

What about Islam? From the very beginning of Islam, Muhammad encouraged the believers to come together for worship. It was understood, however, that prayers were private or individual activities, not communal.

In the early days, Muhammad faced severe opposition because of His teachings, which caused Him to flee from Mecca to Medina in 622 AD. At that time, He first asked His followers to build a square building where they could gather for prayers. The place of worship was called a "mosque," a word deriving from the Arabic word *masjid*, meaning "place of ritual prostration," because many of the obligatory prayers require specific movements and prostrations as they are recited.

An important reason for establishing a place of prayer was to teach new believers how to pray. Most of the people in seventh century Arabia were illiterate, including many believers from Jewish and Christian backgrounds. Therefore, the mosque contained a space in which an educated person, or someone who had memorized the obligatory prayers, stood in front of the believers and led them in reciting the prayers and imitating the movements required for certain parts. The individual leading the prayers was called a mullá from the Arabic word *mawla,* meaning "vicar" or "master," and also meaning "The Source or Focus of Imitation." Mullá may also derive from the Hebrew word *mizrahi*, referring to a religious or community leader.

The temples, synagogues, churches and mosques built by various religions were designed to provide a space for worship and administration as well as a place of counsel and safe refuge for individuals. Originally, these buildings were open to all, but over time they became restricted to communal worship for the faithful of each religious community. In this way, communal worship divided people and led to prejudice against others who were not part of the religious community.

This is reflected in current surveys on church attendance conducted to find out whether people are religious or not. What does going to church on Sunday or attending Friday prayers at a mosque have to do with an individual's religious convictions? Can we distinguish between religious affiliation (being an active participant in a religious community) and being religious (believing in God and trying to follow the Holy Scriptures revealed by a particular Messenger of God on one's own)? Who are we to judge another person's relationship with God based on their choice to participate in communal worship or not?

The development of communal worship conducted by a religious leader has often led believers to hand over all religious decisions to the leader because of his or her "expertise." Believers are often discouraged from thinking rationally or asking questions about teachings. In this void of reason, beliefs easily become irrational, as seen in the rise of fundamentalism around the world. Of international concern is the rise of many Islamic ultraconservative political and religious groups such as the Taliban in Afghanistan, al-Qaeda, ISIS (Islamic State of Iraq and Syria), Hezbollah in Lebanon and many others. Some states that appear to sponsor terrorism, such as Iran and Afghanistan, are ruled by Supreme Leaders who consider themselves chosen by God to interpret the Holy Writings of the Qur'án. In the United States, the rise of militant ultra-right and white supremacist groups often spawned from religious foundations has led to insurrection.

The Advancement of Humanity

Humanity's advancement is impossible without a change from old and outdated views and rules to new and more functional ones. All ideas and thoughts that have brought new understanding to humanity have been the result of new ways of thinking. As humanity evolves and strengthens its ability for rational thinking, can we expect that the need for collective worship and attachment to old culture will be less important or even obsolete? If divisive religious practices persist, ignorance and irrational beliefs will continue to plague humanity.

There is a big difference between ignorance and stupidity. Ignorance can easily be remedied by acquiring knowledge, but stupidity is incurable and characterized by an inability to learn, which, as some have said, allows one to repeat the same mistake hoping for a different outcome.

> Briefly, intelligible realities such as the praiseworthy attributes and perfections of man are purely good and have a positive existence. Evil is simply their non-existence. So ignorance is the want of knowledge, error is the want of guidance, forgetfulness is the want of remembrance, foolishness is the want of understanding: All these are nothing in themselves and have no positive existence.[168]

168 'Abdu'l-Bahá, *Some Answered Questions*, p. 264

To remove all the divisions based on religious beliefs and practices of the past, the Bahá'í concept of worship has revealed a new way of thinking. Throughout the world, Houses of Worship have been constructed. Each of these has a central dome, which represents the unity of all humanity, and nine sides with doors leading out to beautiful gardens and other buildings that serve humanity such as hospitals and schools. All doors are open to every person no matter what their religious belief or affiliation. Everyone is welcome inside to worship God in silence. Essentially, worship remains a personal connection between the individual and God.

> The reason why privacy hath been enjoined in moments of devotion is this, that thou mayest give thy best attention to the remembrance of God, that thy heart may at all times be animated with His Spirit, and not be shut out as by a veil from thy Best Beloved. Let not thy tongue pay lip service in praise of God while thy heart be not attuned to the exalted Summit of Glory, and the Focal Point of communion.[169]

> Whoso reciteth, in the privacy of his chamber, the verses revealed by God, the scattering angels of the Almighty shall scatter abroad the fragrance of the words uttered by his mouth, and cause the heart of every righteous man to throb. Though he may, at first, remain unaware of its effect, yet the virtue of the grace vouchsafed unto him must needs sooner or later exercise its influence upon his soul.[170]

The principle of personal worship may serve to eliminate any remaining tendency to divide and judge others based on

---

169 The Báb, *Selections from the Writings of the Báb*, pp. 93-94.
170 Bahá'u'lláh, *Gleanings from the Writings of Bahá'u'lláh*, CXXXVI.

their professed devotion to God. Over the centuries, individuals, groups and nations have always desired to exalt themselves above others. What would happen if this attitude of superiority were replaced by humility and full acceptance of everyone? Bahá'ís around the world believe the result will be the unity and lasting peace of humanity.

Worship services may be held in a Bahá'í House of Worship, and some individuals, young and old, female and male, will be asked to read or sing selections from the Holy Writings of all religions. These are purely services of worship without sermons or speeches. Daily, devotional meetings are held and on Holy Days there are special programs. The purpose of each House of Worship and its surrounding buildings is to unite everyone in worship and in service to humanity.

Will God Solve Our Problems?

A powerful motivation for joining a religious community is to gain a support network for those times when we face crises. We get multiple viewpoints on solutions and, some believe, the amplified power of group prayer to influence God into providing support.

Why is it that people so often depend on others to make decisions for them instead of pursuing solutions for themselves? When situations get really bad and friends or family cannot help, why do we call out to God or a Higher Power to come to our aid? Are we truly desperate, or are we just so lazy that we hope God will provide the solution for our dilemma? We pray, beg, and beseech. We perform prostrations or movements or traditional dances to reinforce our appeal to the Creator, our heavenly Father, so that He will intervene on our behalf. Even those who believe there is no God find themselves calling on Him in times of dire need. As it has often been said, "In foxholes, there are no atheists."

Rationally, we all know we are but a speck of dust in the universe. No matter how grave our problems may seem, there are many others whose challenges are far greater. Every day, many children struggle to survive hunger and illness. What gives us the right to think that we are more worthy of God's help than such innocent children? Some of our appeals for help are like a lyric sung by Janis Joplin: "O Lord, won't you buy me a Mercedes Benz? My friends all drive Porsches, I must make amends." Even with our limited understanding of the spiritual world, we can see that our Creator may be affecting our lives to reach outcomes that reflect His Will for humanity. Such inexplicable events could be called "miracles," and some have often been associated with the coming of each Messenger of God.

Consider the likelihood of a Jewish child named Moses with a severe stutter who became a great orator and led the Hebrews out of bondage into the Promised Land. Consider a poor, young carpenter who was born with the stigma of being fatherless becoming the Christ, the Anointed One, of the Jewish people. Or consider the illiterate young orphan raised by desert nomads who became Muhammad and was given the gift of such eloquence that his Arabic became one of the most poetic world languages.

The influence of God in the life of humanity can also be viewed from another perspective. Consider a mural that illustrates the epic story of humanity. The painter does not worry about every stroke being in just the right place or being exactly the right color. Of greatest importance is that the finished painting conveys the story in sufficient detail for us to see our history and how situations have been repeated as humanity progresses to a higher existence.

Humanity's growth is like a corkscrew spiraling upward as humanity develops and matures. Yet, due to everyone's dual character as both a material and a spiritual being, certain events repeat themselves. God's Will and our free will can be functioning at the same time. We are born into this life on Earth, and the river of life, which is God's Will, moves us forward.

Many choices in life, however, are the result of our free will and reflect our rational thinking. Some problems we encounter can easily be solved, but others are more challenging. When problems are easy, we only need to reflect and use our rational mind to resolve the issues. By using our mind and imagination to analyze various solutions and control our emotions, we can usually find reasonable solutions. Three steps are needed to successfully solve such problems—obtaining knowledge, harnessing one's will, and taking action. If any one of these three steps is missing, the result can be failure. Unfortunately, the third step—individual and collective action—is too often set aside, to be replaced by prayer in the hopes that such action will not be necessary.

Other kinds of problems can also occur. For example, a severe drought can cause farmers to lose their entire harvest. What can be done about that? Such problems may occur several times in our lives, and sometimes they are beyond the power of an individual to solve. And yet, the three steps—knowledge, will, and action—can still be applied. Knowledge of the cause of a problem is necessary to make predictions about possible future repetitions so we can prepare for them.

In many cases, individuals alone cannot solve a problem. Many of the world's problems are of this type. People must then come together and find the collective will to cooperatively find and execute long-term solutions. Such collective action is urgently needed currently to address the environmental crisis of our planet.

Yet another kind of problem is the death of a friend or loved one. No individual or group can resolve this kind of challenge. Each culture or religious community deals with death in its own way. Some individuals regard death as their own loss and grieve through a tradition of loud crying and weeping, even beating and injuring themselves. However, none of these behaviors can resolve the death of a loved one.

Problems that cannot be solved by individuals or groups, such as chronic illness and death, need to be understood rationally. We all know that illness and death are inevitable, yet in most societies these topics are rarely discussed openly or before a crisis occurs. We realize the difficulties and sadness of life without our loved one, so it's natural to feel personal pain. If we believe there is no existence beyond this life, then death is surely a great loss for both us and the departed. Our grief is doubled.

If we understand that this life is transitory and unpredictable yet there is a beautiful world to come, the fear of dying can be replaced by the serenity of our transition to that new world. However, nothing in our material life can prepare us for that event. Only our spiritual nature can help us cope with it.

All of the Messengers of God have alluded to the freedom and happiness that awaits each of us in the next world. This life, we are told, is like a school in which we learn to use our talents and skills to solve problems and establish loving relationships with others. The knowledge and wisdom we acquire prepares us for our physical death in this world and our spiritual birth into a new existence.

The most reliable sources of knowledge about the afterlife are the Holy Writings of the Messengers of God, which open our eyes and minds to the beauty of the world to come.

With this understanding, a wise person can prepare for the coming of the inevitable death of a loved one and greatly reduce the shock and pain. One can focus instead on a life well lived, rather than the loss now felt.

When Albert Einstein was dying and someone asked how he was preparing for death, he replied, "I will never die, since my thoughts and ideas are all shared with everyone." This was his way of saying that the reality of man is his thoughts, not his physical being. Our thoughts are not bound by time. You may disagree, but Einstein believed in an existence beyond life and into infinity.

Man is possessed of the emanations of consciousness; he has perception, ideality and is capable of discovering the mysteries of the universe. All the industries, inventions and facilities surrounding our daily life were at one time hidden secrets of nature, but the reality of man penetrated them and made them subject to his purposes. According to nature's laws they should have remained latent and hidden; but man, having transcended those laws, discovered these mysteries and brought them out of the plane of the invisible into the realm of the known and visible. How wonderful is the spirit of man![171]

The reality of Christ was always in heaven and will always be. This is the intention of the text of the Gospel. For while Jesus Christ walked upon the earth, He said, "The Son of Man is in heaven." Therefore, holding to literal interpretation and visible fulfillment of the text of the Holy Books is simply imitation of ancestral forms and beliefs; for when we perceive the reality of Christ, these texts and statements become clear and perfectly reconcilable with each other.[172]

The courage, the resolution, the pure motive, the selfless love of one people for another—all the spiritual and moral qualities required for effecting this momentous step towards peace are focused on the will to act. And it is towards arousing the necessary volition that earnest consideration must be given to the reality of man, namely, his thought.[173]

---

171 'Abdu'l-Bahá, *The Promulgation of Universal Peace*.

172 'Abdu'l-Bahá, *The Promulgation of Universal Peace*.

173 "The Promise of World Peace," Message from the Universal House of Justice to the peoples of the world, October 1985.

Nothing in this section should be construed to mean that feelings and emotions are not important. Humans are not robots or computers bereft of feelings. We mean only that our approach to life as mature humans must be based on rational thinking, which leads to knowledge and wisdom, just as irrational thinking perpetuates ignorance and blind faith.

Chapter 9:
Suffering and Prayer

Reliance on God to solve our problems, as discussed in the previous chapter, may seem for many to be a demonstration of faith, but sometimes it is used as an excuse not to personally act to solve our problems. In some cases, it only demonstrates blind faith and insecurity about our own ability to solve problems and endure hardships. Many times, it can be a way of caving into difficulties that we do not want to face and deflecting the many tests of life for fear of pain or failure. In modern society, the concepts of suffering and prayer have become interwoven. Prayer has become a convenient way for many people to deflect their own responsibilities by handing them off to God.

Every day, it seems, we are beleaguered by troubles of all kinds. Life hands us these trying tests and difficulties many times over. The most recent Divine Educator praised those who patiently endure these tests and trials:

> Blessed are the steadfastly enduring, they that are patient under ills and hardships, who lament not over anything that befalleth them, and who tread the path of resignation.[174]

---

174 Bahá'u'lláh, *The Summons of the Lord of Hosts.*

But who among us has the strength and courage to meet such a high standard? And why should we have to withstand such suffering?

The Purpose of Suffering

Suffering has a purpose. Our most recent wisdom tradition provides Teachings that help us recognize tests and difficulties as an expected part of life—inevitable obstacles we each encounter on the path to becoming a better person.

> The more difficulties one sees in the world the more perfect one becomes. The more you plow and dig the ground the more fertile it becomes. The more you cut the branches of a tree the higher and stronger it grows. The more you put the gold in the fire the purer it becomes. The more you sharpen the steel by grinding the better it cuts. Therefore, the more sorrows one sees the more perfect one becomes. That is why, in all times, the Prophets of God have had tribulations and difficulties to withstand. The more often the captain of a ship is in the tempest and difficult sailing the greater his knowledge becomes. Therefore, I am happy that you have had great tribulations and difficulties. ... Strange it is that I love you and still I am happy that you have sorrows.[175]

This physical life, it seems, is a workshop in which we are given the opportunity to grow spiritually through tests. It is human nature to avoid the pain and suffering that results from tests and difficulties, but logically, if we somehow avoid these tests, we may retard our spiritual development. Do not the greatest athletes seek the hardest competitions?

The inevitable tests and difficulties we face are not God's punishments but opportunities for growth. God does not deliver

---

175 'Abdu'l-Baha, *Star of the West.*

them to us, though we often blame Him; rather, all difficulties arise from the material world, not the spiritual realm.

> If we suffer it is the outcome of material things, and all the trials and troubles come from this world of illusion.
>
> For instance, a merchant may lose his trade and depression ensues. A workman is dismissed and starvation stares him in the face. A farmer has a bad harvest, anxiety fills his mind. A man builds a house which is burnt to the ground and he is straightway homeless, ruined, and in despair.
>
> All these examples are to show you that the trials which beset our every step, all our sorrow, pain, shame and grief, are born in the world of matter; whereas the spiritual Kingdom never causes sadness.[176]

Prayer and Meditation

Prayer has usually been understood as communication between humanity and the Divine. Prayer is most often associated with giving thanks to God for what He has provided. The person praying is free to ask God for whatever his heart desires so long as he or she asks God directly with no proxy or intermediary.

> O thou who art turning thy face to God! Close thy eyes to all things else, and open them to the realm of the All-Glorious. Ask whatsoever thou wishest of Him alone; seek whatsoever thou sleekest from Him along.[177]

Though we can ask for whatever we want, we are told that we must submit our desires to the Will of God, which takes precedence.

---

176 'Abdu'l-Bahá, *Paris Talks*.
177 'Abdu'l-Bahá, *Selections from the Writings of 'Abdu'l-Bahá*, 22.

> We must never prefer our wills to the Will of God.[178]

> It behoveth the servant to pray to and seek assistance from God, and to supplicate and implore His aid. Such becometh the rank of servitude, and the Lord will decree whatsoever He desireth, in accordance with His consummate wisdom.[179]

It is always possible that, being human, we may use this acceptance of God's Will in the wrong way. If a problem persists after asking God to solve it, we may simply say, "This is my destiny," or "It must be the Will of God," thereby missing the opportunity to solve the problem rationally, an act for which humans have been well-equipped.

Solving a problem, of course, does not necessarily mean that the problem will go away externally. It can mean that internally we have made peace with the problem, which is the true solution. If we pray for the well-being of a sick friend or family member and they get better, it is obvious that other illnesses or accidents will follow, and death eventually will occur. So, when we pray for physical healing, we should understand that we are really praying for a temporary solution.

In many cultures, we see individuals embark on new business enterprises without proper education or a well-developed plan. When the enterprise fails, the founder concludes that the failure was "the Will of God." This sounds as much like blame as acceptance.

Meditation, which is a wonderful companion to prayer, helps strengthen the human spirit.

> The spirit of man is itself informed and strengthened during meditation; through it affairs of which man knew nothing are unfolded before his view.[180]

---

178 Bahá'u'lláh, *Gleanings from the Writings of Bahá'u'lláh*.
179 'Abdu'l-Bahá, *Prayer, Meditation and the Devotional Attitude*.
180 'Abdu'l-Bahá, *Paris Talks*.

> Through the faculty of meditation man attains to eternal life; through it he receives the breath of the Holy Spirit— the bestowal of the Spirit is given in reflection and meditation.[181]

Whereas prayer is a conversation with the Divine, meditation is a dialogue with oneself.

> It is an axiomatic fact that while you meditate you are speaking with your own spirit. In that state of mind you put certain questions to your spirit and the spirit answers: the light breaks forth and the reality is revealed. In that state of mind you put certain questions to your spirit and the spirit answers: the light breaks forth and the reality is revealed.[182]

The Patterns of Prayer

In studying the patterns of prayer as they evolved over time, we find that prayer in the Old Testament was usually conducted by a religious leader who prayed on behalf of his people. These prayers more often were for the betterment of the faithful and not anyone else. In a few recorded instances, a religious leader even prayed that his personal desires would be fulfilled. As the leader of the Jewish clan, King David prayed for personal preservation.

> Hear my prayer, O LORD, and let my cry come unto thee. Hide not thy face from me in the day when I am in trouble; incline thine ear unto me: in the day when I call answer me speedily. For my days are consumed like smoke, and my bones are burned as an hearth. My heart is smitten and withered like grass...[183]

---

181 'Abdu'l-Bahá, *Paris Talks*.
182 'Abdu'l-Bahá, *Paris Talks*.
183 *Bible*, Psalms 102:1–4

Finally, after this plea for his own security, David beseeched God to preserve the well-being of the nation of Israel.

> But you, O LORD, shall endure forever, And the remembrance of Your name to all generations. You will arise and have mercy on Zion, For the time to favor her, Yes, the set time, has come.[184]

There are numerous "prayers" in the Old Testament in which the Divinity is implored to fulfill personal desires so that the betterment of the faithful could be furthered. Yet in the New Testament there seems to be a change in the purpose of praying. Prayers are more often for the general good and the Cause of Christ than for personal needs.

> But we will give ourselves continually to prayer, and to the ministry of the word.[185]

> Be careful for nothing; but in everything by prayer and supplication with thanksgiving let your requests be made known unto God. And the peace of God, which passeth all understanding, shall keep your hearts and minds through Christ Jesus.[186]

> He that turneth away his ear from hearing the law, even his prayer shall be abomination.[187]

> What then? notwithstanding, every way, whether in pretense, or in truth, Christ is preached; and I therein

---

184 *Bible,* Psalms 102:12–13
185 *Bible,* Acts 6:4
186 *Bible,* Philippians 4:6
187 *Bible,* Proverbs 28:9

do rejoice, yea, and will rejoice. For I know that this shall turn to my salvation through your prayer, and the supply of the Spirit of Jesus Christ.[188]

And the prayer of faith shall save the sick, and the Lord shall raise him up; and if he have committed sins, they shall be forgiven him. Confess your faults one to another, and pray one for another, that ye may be healed. The effectual fervent prayer of a righteous man availeth much."[189]

There are only three recorded prayers of Jesus in the New Testament, and all of them are for the benefit of others or the Cause of Christ, Who was believed to be the savior for humanity. In the first example, Jesus revealed a prayer as a template for His followers.

After this manner therefore pray ye: Our Father which art in heaven, hallowed be thy name. Thy kingdom come, Thy will be done in earth, as it is in heaven. Give us this day our daily bread. And forgive us our trespasses, as we forgive those who trespass against us. And lead us not into temptation, but deliver us from evil: For thine is the kingdom, and the power, and the glory, forever. Amen.[190]

In the second prayer of Jesus, we see His human side, through which He feels pain and anxiety and knows what is about to befall Him. And yet, even as He expresses His trepidation, He unselfishly acknowledges the supremacy of God's Will by using the words, "not my will, but thine, be done" in His prayer:

---

188 *Bible,* Philippians 1:19
189 *Bible,* James 5:16.
190 *Bible,* Matthew 6:10-13.

> Father, if thou be willing, remove this cup from me: nevertheless not my will, but thine, be done." And there appeared an angel unto him from heaven, strengthening him. And being in an agony he prayed more earnestly: and his sweat was as it were great drops of blood falling down to the ground.[191]

The final recorded prayer of Jesus is a selfless prayer of forgiveness for His tormenters.

> When they came to the place called The Skull, they crucified Him there, along with the criminals, one on His right and the other on His left. Then Jesus said, "Father, forgive them, for they know not what they are doing.[192]

In Islamic Scriptures, certain obligatory prayers revealed by Muhammad are to be repeated five times per day to remind the faithful of virtues emphasized by the Founder. Although certain prayers offered by the Founders of other wisdom traditions required followers to be recited at certain times or on certain occasions, no prayers were specified by any Divine Educator to be said daily until the coming of Islam.

The authors have personally concluded that as the development of humanity is now concluding its adolescence, the very act of prayer seems to have changed significantly. The purpose of praying has shifted from seeking universal well-being to imploring God to fulfill personal needs and wants. Since most of the world's population can now read and write, individuals have become empowered to say their own prayers. Today, prayer less frequently beseeches the Divine for the good of humanity but seeks to persuade God to abandon natural laws and conform His Will to that of the person praying. In some cases, many people gather to pray for God to do something they

---

191 *Bible*, Luke 22:45.
192 *Bible*, Luke 23.33–34.

want Him to do, as if a larger number of prayers could have greater influence on the Will of God. In many of the national sports, both sides pray to win. How do we expect God to answer the prayers of these fans?

The Ritual of Ritual

When does a prayer become a ritual, a tradition in which its true meaning eventually becomes forgotten, and its only focus is on the repetition of physical movements and words? The type of ritual known as religious action is a solemn ceremony consisting of a series of actions performed according to a prescribed order. Religious rituals can be comforting to some people who rely on the repetitive nature to provide a sense of stability to their lives. But are religious rituals beneficial to a belief system?

Almost all the past wisdom traditions combine elaborate rituals with their prayers, which many contemporary worshipers find hard to accept. About 1700 BC, the Babylonians were sacrificing twelve-year-old virgin girls to satisfy their gods, and various tribes into the twentieth century engaged in human sacrifices, all beseeching their gods to grant them something in return for their sincerity of belief. The Hindus of India use the water of the River Ganges, considered one of the most polluted waterways in the world, to sanctify themselves and their animals from the sins of the day. The unclean Ganges seems like one of the least likely places to cleanse one of sin or anything else.

Humans have a propensity for idolizing rituals of movement or meaningful objects. When God asked Abraham to sacrifice His son to prove loyalty to His covenant with God, the covenant was the focus of importance, and yet it was the Stone of Sacrifice that became the point of adoration within the walls of Jerusalem, obscuring the status of the covenant itself. Later, that Stone was revered by the Christians and then the Muslims until the Prophet of Islam changed the direction of the Center of Adoration from the Stone of Sacrifice to the House of God (Kaaba) in Mecca.

Jewish rituals are many, depending on the tribe or the sect, but the most social ones everyone is familiar with are the repetitious prayer and bowing to the wall in Jerusalem. This may go on for a number of hours depending on the extent of the belief of the faithful and the request for their wishes to be fulfilled by their God.

Roman Catholics have specific rituals that provide guidelines for pageantry and how to stand and approach the front pulpit. There are many rituals for the rosary, baptisms, communion, Ash Wednesday and other commemorative dates requiring believers to be dressed in a certain manner and to ritually light candles for a specific person or thought. No one dares to ask who initiated such rituals. It certainly was not Jesus.

In Islam, many aspects of worship have also become ritualized. The most dynamic and colorful may be the Shi'a commemoration of the martyrdom of Imam Husayn, the son of Alí, who was betrayed and finally killed in the outskirts of Kofi in Iraq. Every year during Muharram (meaning "forbidden"), the first month of the Islamic lunar calendar, this act of deception and martyrdom is memorialized for a few days called the Days of Ashura & Tashura.

During these days, numerous believers mourn, beating and flagellating themselves to prove their dedication to this sect of Islam. It is a disturbing scene of self-induced violence for those who do not share in the beliefs. Many can be seen carrying on such violent behavior. They cut themselves and march in the streets chanting rhythmic poems to the beating of drums. While this is a dramatic and, some would say, grotesque display of dedication and prayer, it is also a mesmerizing show for onlookers.

Women Muslims often hold special prayer sessions in black clothing at which a male from the religious house, called Madoh, repeats the tragic story of Imam Husain's martyrdom while the audience members beat themselves and cry aloud to show the depth of their mourning. Devout Muslims have told us that they have more gatherings for crying and beating themselves than for any joyful occasion.

Repeatedly, the Divine Educators have warned against the misuse of rituals, reminding us that they become the center of adoration, which overwhelms the importance of the original meaning. In the Old Testament, Moses did more than warn the Israelites of these dangers; He instigated a rebellion against the rituals of Egypt, which ultimately freed the Hebrews. Perhaps the main reason Jesus overthrew the money changers of the temple was to show that the ritual of exchanging Roman money for Jewish money for donation to the temple deviated from the true belief system.

We need to ask what part of our religious ceremonies have become rituals that carry no meaning except as a public show of faith, which in some views is a cause of segregation. When we perform rituals without thinking or reflecting on the meaning of them, it is as though we have become robots following a scripted performance to show onlookers the depth of our devotion.

And yet, we have been told that the purpose of prayer is not meant to be a public display but something more intimate and meaningful.

> The wisdom of prayer is this: That it causeth a connection between the servant and the True One, because in that state man with all heart and soul turneth his face towards His Highness the Almighty, seeking His association and desiring His love and compassion. The greatest happiness for a lover is to converse with his beloved, and the greatest gift for a seeker is to become familiar with the object of his longing; that is why with every soul who is attracted to the Kingdom of God, his greatest hope is to find an opportunity to entreat and supplicate before his Beloved, appeal for His mercy and grace and be immersed in the ocean of His utterance, goodness and generosity...[193]

---

193 'Abdu'l-Bahá, *Tablets of 'Abdu'l-Bahá 'Abbás* vol. 1-3

But we ask for things which the divine wisdom does not desire for us, and there is no answer to our prayer. His wisdom does not sanction what we wish. We pray, "O God! Make me wealthy!" If this prayer were universally answered, human affairs would be at a standstill. There would be none left to work in the streets, none to till the soil, none to build, none to run the trains. "Therefore, it is evident that it would not be well for us if all prayers were answered. The affairs of the world would be interfered with, energies crippled and progress hindered. But whatever we ask for which is in accord with divine wisdom, God will answer. Assuredly!

For instance, a very feeble patient may ask the doctor to give him food which would be positively dangerous to his life and condition. He may beg for roast meat. The doctor is kind and wise. He knows it would be dangerous to his patient so he refuses to allow it. The doctor is merciful; the patient, ignorant. Through the doctor's kindness the patient recovers; his life is saved. Yet the patient may cry out that the doctor is unkind, not good, because he refuses to answer his pleading.

God is merciful. In His mercy He answers the prayers of all His servants when according to His supreme wisdom it is necessary.[194]

In one sense, we can say that prayer has become a means of communication between the lover and the Beloved (the Divine) and that humanity has come of age to experience true love in which only loyalty and fidelity exist.

How many times, we wonder, have people told a friend about a problem they were having only to be told by that friend, "I'll pray about that for you." We would never doubt the sincerity of a friend to

---

194 'Abdu'l-Bahá, *The Promulgation of Universal Peace*, pp. 245-247

assist with prayer, and many may appreciate the offer. Nevertheless we wonder how that friend had determined that God would be more responsive to his or her prayer than to the prayer from the person with the problem. We also wonder if that friend had ever considered how the other person might interpret his offer of prayer, suggesting as it did that it might be more effective, the tipping point for God's decision to fulfill or not fulfill the request.

If all the requests for healing were granted, only atheists would ever die. If all the requests for financial aid were granted by God, governments would have to print a lot more money, and we would have massive inflation. Rationally, the main purpose of prayer cannot be to get stuff from God but to become, through prayer and meditation, better persons who are more spiritually developed and capable of bringing about an ever-advancing civilization.

Prayer, when intended as personal communication with the Divine, should remain personal and reserved for intimate settings. The purpose of all the Divine Educators has been to unite mankind and not to introduce actions and rituals that would separate us from each other. In the end, prayer itself can become an empty ritual for people of all Faiths if not said with sincerity.

> Take heed lest excessive reading and too many acts of piety in the daytime and in the night season make you vainglorious. Should a person recite but a single verse from the Holy Writings in a spirit of joy and radiance, this would be better for him than reciting wearily all the Scriptures of God... Recite ye the verses of God in such measure that ye be not overtaken with fatigue or boredom. Burden not your souls so as to cause exhaustion and weigh them down, but rather endeavour to lighten them, that they may soar on the wings of revealed Verses unto the dawning-place of His signs.[195]

---

195 Bahá'u'lláh, *Kitáb-i-Aqdás,*

Chapter 10:
Prejudice and Blind Faith

We Are All Guilty

Talk with any number of people, and if you listen intently, you will learn that almost no one is free from all prejudices. We all possess some biases and blind faith about a few things. But it is extremely difficult, perhaps impossible, to see prejudice exhibited in our own speech, behavior and emotional responses. In a sense, even the simple act of comparing ourselves to another person or group can be a sign of prejudice. Yes, we all have some prejudices, whether ethnic, national, political, religious, racial, social or economic.

If we tried to find evidence of prejudice or blind faith in our thoughts and actions, most of us would come up empty, while the people close to us could probably compile a list of our petty biases. It's easy to think we are above prejudice and too rational to have blind faith in anything.

There have been numerous studies about these kinds of negative stereotypes that we hold in ourselves but are not consciously aware of. The possession of these invisible biases is called implicit prejudice. Steven C. Hayes, PhD, is a professor of psychology at the University of Nevada, Reno, and is one of the most cited psychologists in the world. In studies of all forms of prejudice, his lab found that they can all be explained by what's called authoritarian distancing—the belief that we are different from a group of "others," and because those "others" are different, they pose a threat that we need to control. Because security is so highly valued, we tend to segregate ourselves from those with even minor differences, which is contrary to the efforts of the Divine Educators to unite us.

Hayes's lab concluded that there were three psychological characteristics that led some people into authoritarian distancing:

- the relative inability to take the perspective of other people;

- the inability to feel the pain of others when you do take their perspective;

- the inability to be emotionally open to the pain of others when you do feel it.[196]

These three psychological characteristics all relate to a lack empathy for others. Empathy is the ability to sense other people's emotions, coupled with the ability to imagine what someone else might be thinking or feeling. Conversely, one might conclude that having or developing empathy might counteract the implicit prejudice we all experience.

Hayes's evidence and other studies show that humans have a predisposition to use prejudice, or something preliminary to it, as a tool for self-preservation. There is safety—at least the feeling of safety—in associating with one's own kind. Differences of appearance, race, even beliefs can signal danger. This, of course, not only gives rise to racial prejudice, but also nationalism, religious persecution, gender injustice, and many more social ills. These tendencies to see most people as "others" and "inferior" is true for Blacks, Whites, American Indians, Papua New Guineans and all minority groups

---

196   https://ideas.ted.com/prejudiced-thoughts-run-through-all-our-minds-the-key-is-what-we-do-with-them/

whether their differences are in behavior, accent, appearance, food preferences or anything else.

The problem is that throughout the world there are infinite variations in every element of appearance. To help us deal with this enormous complexity of features, each one of which could be a cause for prejudice, we try to aggregate people more generally by their looks, beliefs. and cultures. We create broader targets of prejudice called "black and brown people" or "Hispanics" or "Arabs."

If we were animals, this behavior might be logical for self-preservation. But it is illogical since we are human and the reality of humans is their thoughts, not their physical superiority. If we had the time, the process of segmenting and categorizing humans could further be narrowed down until we identified a "pure" population—a group that was as much like us as possible. The Nazis attempted this when they pursued the development of a pure "Aryan" race. Another example is the splitting of various religions into sects identified in many cases by tiny differences in doctrine.

As travel has become easier for more people, the big clusters of like people have dispersed, so it is more difficult to define groups by cultural differences. Segregating them into smaller groups can better serve the needs of prejudice.

One basic problem of prejudice is that when we start judging people based on what we see and hear from them, the information we have about them is limited, so ignorance fills that void with assumptions and unfounded beliefs, which is what prejudice is based upon.

One solution is to realize that there is only one race, the human race, and then evaluate our own activities and thoughts, leaving other people to judge themselves. Self-judgement can cast aside most of our prejudicial veils and help us abandon the pedestal of arrogance to see each individual as a unique spiritual being for whom physical features and cultural behaviors are no longer the basis for our value judgements. When importance is placed on our own rational thinking, most prejudices diminish. This eventually can lead humankind to be more tolerant and stop segmenting people by differences of race, nationality or religion.

Prejudice and Discrimination

Prejudice and discrimination are closely related. In a paper by Will C. van den Hoonaard, "Prejudice is a cultural attitude—a harmful and deeply-rooted paradigm based on negative stereotypes about individuals or groups. Discrimination is the active denial of desired goals from a category of persons."[197] These categories can be based on sex, ethnicity, nationality, religion, language, class, gender, age and even physical or mental disabilities. Prejudice, then, is what we believe about certain groups of people. Discrimination is what we do based on our beliefs about them. Do we segregate them from the broader society, shun them socially or restrict their rights?

No society or nation has been immune to prejudice and discrimination either as victim or victimizer. Contemporary forms of these evils date back to European colonization that transformed previously isolated societies. Extreme forms of too-familiar discrimination include genocide, slavery, apartheid, discriminatory immigration laws, restrictive voting laws, disenfranchisement, female genital mutilation, rape culture... the list is obscenely long. Certain groups, such as Jews (as in anti-Semitism) and the Roma (pejoratively known as Gypsies), seem to suffer more persistently than others from discrimination regardless of time and place.

There is no universally accepted theory of the causes of prejudice and discrimination, but most scholars agree that humans are not born with these outrageous and harmful paradigms even if they are genetically predisposed to develop prejudices later when threatened. Considerable evidence exists showing that prejudice is absent in young children.[198] If prejudice and discrimination were inherent in

---

197 Will C. van den Hoonaard, "Prejudice and Discrimination."
198 Allport, Gordon W. (1958) *The Nature of Prejudice.*

humans, it would be difficult to account for all the intermarriage and assimilation among highly differentiated human groups.

Clearly, prejudice fits all the definitions of a paradigm or way of thinking. And as we've seen, when one is inside a paradigm it is nearly impossible to see the paradigm that imprisons one. To break free from the accretion of old ideas and rules of behavior often requires an "aha" moment, an epiphany, a bulldozer of fresh thinking that flattens the ruts of superstition and blind faith that created artificial boundaries for our thinking.

This, we believe, is the work of the Divine Educator.

Herd Instinct

In most discussions with others, why do we tend to avoid talking about religion and political affiliations? Most people have stayed in the same religion, even the specific sect as their parents, even if they do not attend the same place of worship. Is this because they have undertaken an independent investigation of truth to ensure that they believe what their religion teaches, or is it a kind of blind faith? There is a strong pull, of course, for children to remain in the family's religion or political party. Few want to be the "black sheep" in the family and have to live with the perpetual disdain of loved ones.

If we are rational and have carefully considered the alternatives in religion and politics, why do we feel uncomfortable talking objectively about these subjects? Can we avoid exposing prejudices by not talking about things that may betray them? Do we want to avoid assigning responsibility for social problems to our own culture or religion or political party? Do we fear that speaking out will imply that we consider ourselves better than our friends?

We are all capable of thinking rationally, yet we avoid talking about matters of belief because so many of our beliefs have little or no rational basis. We have been taught to believe many things based purely on the traditions and interpretations of our forefathers rather than our own logical thinking and independent investigation.

Most of us rely on rational thinking to resolve issues for our personal well-being, but seldom consider how easily we can alienate others. We tend to have a "herd instinct," which urges us to form relationships with co-religionists, political buddies, neighbors, friends and other peer groups comprised of people with similar educational or financial status. We like to join groups even if the thinking of members does not match ours. We have been taught the importance of being accepted in society, so we do our best to win the friendship and trust of friends and acquaintances at school, in our workplaces and in our neighborhoods. Nobody wants to be an outsider, yet we are all outsiders to a degree because we do not totally share each other's way of thinking. Nevertheless, being accepted into a group is an important part of the herd instinct. Instead, if we nurtured our own free thinking, how would it affect our uniqueness and our talents? Does independent thinking contribute to the advancement of an individual as well as a society?

If we continually conform to the thinking of the herd, we perpetuate a culture of ignorance. Ignorance causes fear of those who are perceived as different from us and is the basis of all prejudices. On the one hand, we may promote freedom of speech, freedom of religion and freedom of thought in matters of politics. On the other hand, herd thinking may cause us to feel superior to others and desire to be different and perhaps more "correct" than a competitive group. Such thinking may even cause destructive and irrational behaviors that we may not have performed if we had been alone.

For example, if we profess a religious affiliation—Jewish, Christian, Muslim or any other wisdom tradition—are we suggesting that we are better than those who are not part of that group? The word Jew or Jewish is the name of an ethnoreligious group or nation originating in the region of Judah in ancient Palestine. The word Christian is the name given to people who follow the teachings of Christ. The word Islam derives from a word meaning "submission to the Will of God." Thus, the merit of the followers of Islam—who are called Muslims—is based on their deeds and the degree to which they demonstrate submission to the Will of God judged only by the Divine Educator.

However, since religious teachings have been revealed for the spiritual development of all humanity, is it still necessary to divide humanity into different groups with different names depending on which Messenger of God they choose to follow? Do such divisions imply that one group is better than another, even when the true source of their knowledge is the same?

Would it not be more appropriate to be known by one's deeds rather than the name of the Divine Educator whose teachings one strives to follow? The worship of God and the beliefs we follow are very personal matters. Would it make more sense, then, for one to say he has entered the school of Christ or the school of Muhammad?

The knowledge to be gained in such schools is infinite, therefore no one can claim to be all-knowing. No one could claim the authority to interpret the Holy Scriptures for others or dictate to them how to apply those teachings in their lives. Instead, all would be encouraged to read and study the Holy Scriptures for themselves and use their rational thinking to follow those teachings. In effect, no one would ever graduate from these schools. Instead, learning would become a lifelong process.

As the latest generation of humanity, we must continue to correct what is needed to reach the goal of the unity of humankind.

> Be anxiously concerned with the needs of the age ye live in, and center your deliberations on its exigencies and requirements." The transformation in the way that great numbers of ordinary people are coming to see themselves—a change that is dramatically abrupt in the perspective of the history of civilization—raises fundamental questions about the role assigned to the general body of humanity in the planning of our planet's future.[199]

---

199 "The Prosperity of Humankind," Baha'i International Community, Of-

Overcoming Prejudices

For centuries, one of the most challenging issues facing humanity has been the issue of racial prejudice. Over past centuries in the United States, racial prejudice has targeted black- and brown-skinned peoples beginning with the extermination of American Indians and the enslavement of Africans, then expanding in the last two centuries to discrimination based on the origin of one's ancestors. All such prejudices are the result of ignorance about others and are fueled by fear of those who are different.

Other kinds of prejudice are no less destructive to human dignity and life. Whole populations have been displaced by wars and famine, forcing people to live in new and strange places where they are neither understood nor accepted. Different opportunities in life have led to varying social and economic conditions, and eventually to different classes of society—rich and poor, educated and illiterate.

For centuries, women have suffered discrimination and oppression throughout the world, and in many cases their station is only good for propagation and serving the needs of men. Sadly, this attitude toward women has been manifested in Jewish, Christian and Muslim traditions based on pagan traditions as well as misinterpretations of the Holy Scriptures. Sons have been considered superior to daughters. Men have been granted rights and responsibilities denied to women, especially equal opportunities for education and training.

Men have been allowed a voice in decision-making, whereas women were excluded and expected to keep silent. This guidance, for example, was given to the early Christian churches by Paul, a former Jew, who perpetuated the prejudices against women held by the Jewish community:

> **Let your women keep silence in the churches: for it is not permitted unto them to speak; but they are com-**

fice of Public Information, p. 3.

> manded to be under obedience, as also saith the law. And if they will learn anything, let them ask their husbands at home: for it is a shame for women to speak in the church.[200]

Now, in the twenty-first century, men in some parts of the world continue to deny equal access to education for girls and women out of fear that educated women will not be subservient and submissive to men. In extreme cases, daughters are treated as property and sold to others as perpetual servants or child brides when they are younger than fifteen years of age, or they are given in marriage to repay the debts of their father. All such abuses are based on a lack of basic education, misinterpretations of religious teachings and intractable paradigms that hold both men and women captive.

For generations, people have been blindly imitating their forefathers, who have trained them according to the dogma or laws of their particular religious affiliation. Such blind imitation reinforces learned paradigms and is a cause of prejudice.

> The greatest cause of bereavement and disheartening in the world of humanity is ignorance based on blind imitations... the foundations of the divine religions are one and the same. The differences which have arisen between us are due to blind imitations of dogmatic beliefs and adherence to ancestral forms of worship... These blind imitations and hereditary prejudices have invariably become the cause of bitterness and hatred and have filled the world with darkness and violence of war... The religious differences and divisions which exist in the world are due to blind imitations of forms without knowledge or investigation of the fundamental divine reality which underlies all the religions.[201]

---

200 *Bible*, 1 Corinthians 14: 34-35
201 Abdu'l-Bahá, *The Promulgation of Universal Peace*, pp. 291, 403, 180, 287.

Imagine what our world would be like if all the prejudices of the past, all those vestigial remnants of our inhumanity, were to continue. Would these outdated thoughts and actions promote the advancement of humanity? Would there be greater unity within families, among neighbors or even between nations?

If not, would the world become even more afflicted with discord, conflict and the deterioration of any progress that has been achieved in each society? In what kind of society do we want our children to be raised and educated? Can we work together to eliminate all the prejudices of the past and bring about a new way of life where every human is appreciated for their uniqueness as a member of the human race?

To break free from the prejudices of the past, we must encourage and enable everyone to independently investigate the truth of every matter. A basic education and commitment to research and analysis of issues are needed to overcome the seemingly ingrained habit of blind imitation. This requires an attitude of curiosity and a desire to learn, as well as courage and perseverance. As Jesus said some two thousand years ago:

> **Ask, and it shall be given you; seek, and ye shall find; know, and it shall be opened unto you.**[202]

When every person is encouraged and trained to think independently and have a thirst for learning and knowledge, humanity will be freed from the darkness of ignorance. Instead of continually repeating the errors of the past, humanity will develop new knowledge and understanding. Knowledge will become the distinguishing feature of a new global society noted for its unity in diversity. The realization of the unity or oneness of all humanity will promote a new way of acting toward our fellow human beings.

All have been created by the same God, who is like a loving

---

202 *Bible*, Mathew 7:7.

Father and cares for each and every person without favoring one more than another. God's love for humanity can be compared to the sun and its life-giving rays, which provide warmth and light for everything on Earth. The rays of the sun stream down to Earth and benefit all. No distinction is made between people, whether their lives are sinful or angelic, regardless of their skin color or ethnic background or religious affiliation. Some Holy Writings call these rays of the Sun "the grace and bounty of God." Each individual has the opportunity and privilege to benefit from these bounties.

At the same time, no one can force anyone to accept these beliefs. No one has the right to judge another on their progress in life. Each person has unique talents and capacities. For example, one person may have musical or artistic talents, another may have strengths in mathematics and abstract thinking while others are great in sports. We are able to assess the performance of others and their acquired abilities. However, we cannot fully know the potential or capacity of another person, and in this regard no one can pass judgement on another. We can only hope to judge our own efforts to achieve our full capacity and best performance.

We all know that the life of each individual is very limited. It passes in the twinkling of an eye. How much effort have we made to educate ourselves, to work hard and earn sufficient income to look after our families and our future needs? Beyond satisfying our personal needs, however, what have we done to improve the life of humanity? Every individual can make a difference in this world through their deeds, no matter what their work or other talents.

> **The betterment of the world can be accomplished through pure and goodly deeds, through commendable and seemly conduct.**[203]

---

203 Bahá'u'lláh, cited in *The Advent of Divine Justice*, pp. 24–25.

> Let your acts be a guide unto all mankind, for the professions of most men, be they high or low, differ from their conduct. It is through your deeds that ye can distinguish yourselves from others. Through them the brightness of your light can be shed upon the whole earth.[204]

We should ask ourselves many questions at the end of every day: What did I accomplish today? Were my thoughts and actions rational or reasonable? Could I improve tomorrow? How can my actions serve others in the future—my family, my community, my country, even all of humanity? What if others would act like I did today—what would be the result of such behavior?

In our world of advanced technology and nuclear power, we can no longer blindly follow the traditions of the past. Now is a time of tremendous change for humanity. Whatever leads to division or segregation, fanaticism or hatred must be rooted out. To achieve the long-promised peace on Earth we must eliminate the prejudices of the past and discontinue blind faith in outdated traditions. Now is the time to rely on new insights gained through rational thinking.

---

204 Bahá'u'lláh, *Gleanings from the Writings of Bahá'u'lláh*, CXXXIX, p. 305

Chapter 11:
The Power of Love

Up to now, we have been focusing on the importance of rational thinking to promote the unity and peace of humanity. Humanity possesses another quality or power that is essential to this purpose—the power of love.

We may think that love is just an emotion, a feeling between two people. However, love is a much stronger power. Love is the source of our existence, as stated so beautifully in these Holy Writings:

> O SON OF MAN! Veiled in My immemorial being and in the ancient eternity of My essence, I knew My love for thee; therefore I created thee, have engraved on thee Mine image and revealed to thee My beauty.
>
> O SON OF MAN! I loved thy creation, hence I created thee. Wherefore, do thou love Me, that I may name thy name and fill thy soul with the spirit of life.
>
> O SON OF BEING! Love Me, that I may love thee. If thou lovest Me not, My love can in no wise reach thee. Know this, O servant.

> O SON OF MAN! If thou lovest Me, turn away from thyself; and if thou seekest My pleasure, regard not thine own; that thou mayest die in Me and I may eternally live in thee.[205]

Love Holds the Universe Together

Love is the power of attraction that holds the universe together. The axis around which life revolves is love, while the axis around which death and destruction revolve is animosity and hatred.

Consider the mineral kingdom. Here, if attraction did not exist between the atoms, the composite substance of matter would not be possible. Science has proven that every existent phenomenon is composed of elements and atomic particles. If attraction did not exist between the elements and among the particles, that composition would never have been possible.

For example, a stone is an existent phenomenon—a composition of elements. A bond of attraction has brought them together. Through the cohesion of its ingredients, this stone has been formed. The stone is the lowest degree of phenomena, but within it a power of attraction is manifest without which the stone could not exist. This power of attraction in the mineral world is the only expression of love the stone can manifest.

In the next highest realm of existence, the vegetable kingdom, we see that a plant is the result of cohesion among various elements just as the stone is in the mineral kingdom. But the plant has an additional power—absorption of nutrients from the earth. This higher degree of attraction differentiates the plant from the stone. In the vegetable kingdom, this absorption of nutrients is the highest expression of love the plant possesses. By this power of attraction, the plant grows daily. In its realm of existence, then, love is also the cause of life.

---

205 Bahá'u'lláh, *The Hidden Words of Bahá'u'lláh*, from the Arabic, No. 3,4,5,7.

In the animal kingdom, which is higher in degree than the vegetable realm, the power of love is even more resplendent because the attraction by which elements cohere and cellular atoms commingle reveals itself in emotions and sensibilities that produce instinctive fellowship and association. Animals of the same species are imbued with kindness and affinity for each other—except, perhaps, when rival mates appear.

Finally, in the human realm, we find that many qualities of animals—such as sight, smell, hearing, flying and speed of reaction—are superior to the comparable native qualities of humankind. Humans, however, have overcome these deficiencies by developing microscopes to see the smallest particles that no animal could ever perceive, telescopes to see the far reaches of the universe, microphones to hear the faintest sounds, aircraft and rockets to fly farther and higher. Yet, what really distinguishes humans from animals is that humans possess a rational soul.

> The human spirit which distinguishes man from the animal is the rational soul; and these two names—the human spirit and the rational soul—designate one thing.[206]

Man possesses a degree of attraction that is conscious and spiritual, an immeasurable advance from the animal kingdom. In the human realm, spiritual inclinations surface and love exists to a superlative degree. In the passage below, we learn that this is the cause of life:

> The proof is clear that in all degrees and kingdoms unity and agreement, love and fellowship are the cause of life, whereas dissension, animosity and separation are ever conducive to death. Therefore, we must strive with life and soul in order that day by day unity and

---

206 'Abdu'l-Bahá, *Some Answered Questions*, p. 208.

> agreement may be increased among mankind and that love and affinity may become more resplendently glorious and manifest.[207]

The power of love develops slowly over one's lifetime. As a child, self-love predominates, but with increasing maturity an individual learns the importance of self-sacrifice and service to others.

Although the seed of love as a feeling is from the animal kingdom, it grows to its full capacity within the grounds of the rational soul in humans. This suggests that animals have feelings and can experience attraction, though the animal instincts of survival of their species tend to override all other qualities.

The word "love" is used extensively in Scriptures where it often speaks of a kind of love affair between God and His Creation. In the following passage, the concept of love is described metaphysically and explains how creation is tied to human consciousness:

> There are four kinds of love. The first is the love that flows from God to man; it consists of the inexhaustible graces, the Divine effulgence and heavenly illumination. Through this love the world of being receives life. Through this love man is endowed with physical existence, until, through the breath of the Holy Spirit—this same love—he receives eternal life and becomes the image of the Living God. This love is the origin of all the love in the world of creation.
>
> The second is the love that flows from man to God. This is faith, attraction to the Divine, enkindlement, progress, entrance into the Kingdom of God, receiving the Bounties of God, illumination with the lights of the Kingdom. This love is the origin of all philanthropy; this love causes the hearts of men to reflect the rays of the Sun of Reality.

207 'Abdu'l-Bahá, *The Promulgation of Universal Peace*, pp. 255-257.

The third is the love of God towards the Self or Identity of God. This is the transfiguration of His Beauty, the reflection of Himself in the mirror of His Creation. This is the reality of love, the Ancient Love, the Eternal Love. Through one ray of this Love all other love exists.

The fourth is the love of man for man. The love which exists between the hearts of believers is prompted by the ideal of the unity of spirits. This love is attained through the knowledge of God, so that men see the Divine Love reflected in the heart. Each sees in the other the Beauty of God reflected in the soul, and finding this point of similarity, they are attracted to one another in love. This love will make all men the waves of one sea, this love will make them all the stars of one heaven and the fruits of one tree. This love will bring the realization of true accord, the foundation of real unity.[208]

Humanity collectively is concluding its period of adolescence and going through a transition leading to an age of maturity.[209] As such, the old concepts of reward and punishment should no longer be based on an external heaven and hell but should be realigned in keeping with the close relationship between a parent and a child who has reached the age of maturity. A wise parent counsels children based on the love that exists between them, not on threats or fanciful rewards.

Humanity today, it appears, is expected to play the role of the lover who, with his or her Beloved—the Divine—are now joining to bring humanity to the next level of existence with knowledge and understanding. Therefore, we are no longer externally rewarded with and punished with hell, but rather we are motivated by our

---

208 'Abdu'l-Bahá, *Paris Talks*, Pages 180-181

209 Letter from the Universal House of Justice to the Followers of Bahá'u'lláh in the Democratic Republic of the Congo, 1 November 2022.

intrinsic love of the Divine. The guidance from the Divine is now clothed in love.

> Observe My commandments, for the love of My beauty." Happy is the lover that hath inhaled the divine fragrance of his Best-Beloved from these words, laden with the perfume of a grace which no tongue can describe.[210]

Love often seems to rely more on feelings than rational thinking. Someone in love can be prepared to follow their heart—their emotions—to the point of sacrificing everything for their beloved. A classical Persian poet speaks of someone in love as possessed and dazed:

I am lost, O Love, possessed and dazed,
Love's fool am I, in all the earth.
They call me first among the crazed,
Though I once came first for wit and worth.
O Love, who sellest me this wine,
O Love, for whom I burn and bleed,
Love, for whom I cry and pine -
Thou the Piper, I the reed.
If Thou wishest me to live,
Through me blow Thy holy breath.
The touch of Jesus Thou wilt give
To me, who've lain an age in death.
Thou, both End and Origin,
Thou without and Thou within -
From every eye Thou hidest well,
And yet in every eye dost dwell.[211]

---

210 Bahá'u'lláh, *The Kitab-i-Aqdas (Book of Certitude)*, p. 20

211 The poet Rúmí, quoted in 'Abdu'l-Bahá, *Memorials of the Faithful*, pp. 30-31.

As much as rational thought is needed in social discourse, love is required for the inner peace and happiness of every individual. Love gives meaning to life. Without love, this life becomes meaningless and worthless.

At the highest level, the power of love manifests itself in the relationship between an individual and His Creator. At this level, material or worldly accomplishments become less valued. An individual may willingly give all his possessions, titles and fame for a glimpse of the beauty of his Beloved. The Divine Educators have revealed many verses and prayers imploring God to strengthen the bond of this love:

> Purify me of all that is not of Thee, and strengthen me to love Thee and to fulfill Thy pleasure, that I may delight myself in the contemplation of Thy beauty, and be rid of all attachment to any of Thy creatures, and may, at every moment, proclaim: "Magnified be God, the Lord of the worlds!"[212]

Another reality besides rational thinking, then, also guides humanity. This reality is a frequent theme of the Holy Writings of the Divine Educators. When Jesus was asked by a Jewish lawyer to identify the greatest commandment, He replied...

> Thou shalt love the Lord thy God with all thy heart, and with all thy soul, and with all thy mind. This is the first and great commandment. And the second is like unto it, Thou shalt love thy neighbor as thyself. On these two commandments hang all the law and the prophets.[213]

Poetry is another way to try to describe the beauty of love to our fellow man, our brother and our Creator:

---

212 Bahá'u'lláh, *Prayers and Meditations by Bahá'u'lláh*, p. 126.
213 *Bible*, Mathew 22: 37-40.

Unless ye must,
Bruise not the serpent in the dust,
How much less wound a man.
And if ye can,
No ant should ye alarm,
Much less a brother harm.[214]
If I, like Abraham, through flames must go,
Or yet like John a bloodstained road must run;
If, Joseph-like, Thou'd cast me in a well,
Or shut me up within a prison cell-
Or make me e'en as poor as Mary's Son-
I will not go from Thee,
But ever stand
My soul and body bowed to Thy command.[215]

Such a meaningful and beautiful relationship with one's Creator, however, is not sufficient to bring about the unity of humankind. The inner feelings and experiences of each individual are different, and these differences can lead to division and segregation, which are the opposites of unity. The power of love alone cannot unite all hearts. But when love combines with rational thinking, the power of both is magnified to produce the strongest means for achieving unity and peace.

An Urgent Need

At this point in human history there is an urgent need for a creative power or energy from a higher realm, the divine realm, to provide the guidance necessary for humanity to achieve higher levels of collective thought and reasoning. As mentioned earlier, the second law of thermodynamics states that the physical world moves toward disorder or decomposition unless there is an infusion of energy from an outside force to maintain its organization and structure. All around us, we can see vast evidence of disorder and decomposition. Is it

---

214 'Abdu'l-Bahá, *Selections from the Writings of 'Abdu'l-Bahá*, No. 206, p. 256.
215 'Abdu'l-Bahá, *Selections from the Writings of 'Abdu'l-Bahá*, No. 191, p. 228.

not clear that humanity with no guidance is struggling and cannot advance to a higher level of intellect and reasoning?

God's purpose in sending His Prophets unto men is twofold. The first is to liberate the children of men from the darkness of ignorance, and guide them to the light of true understanding. The second is to ensure the peace and tranquility of mankind, and provide all the means by which they can be established.

The Prophets of God should be regarded as physicians whose task is to foster the well-being of the world and its peoples, that, through the spirit of oneness, they may heal the sickness of a divided humanity... No man, however acute his perception, can ever hope to reach the heights which the wisdom and understanding of the Divine Physician have attained. Little wonder, then, if the treatment prescribed by the physician in this day should not be found to be identical with that which he prescribed before. How could it be otherwise when the ills affecting the sufferer necessitate at every stage of his sickness a special remedy? In like manner, every time the Prophets of God have illumined the world with the resplendent radiance of the Daystar of Divine knowledge, they have invariably summoned its peoples to embrace the light of God through such means as best befitted the exigencies of the age in which they appeared...

These are not days of prosperity and triumph. The whole of mankind is in the grip of manifold ills. Strive, therefore, to save its life through the wholesome medicine which the almighty hand of the unerring Physician hath prepared.[216]

216 Bahá'u'lláh, *Gleanings from the Writings of Bahá'u'lláh*, XXXIV, pp. 79-81.

It becomes clear, then, that the Divine Educators provide the infusion of energy needed at each period in humanity's history. In our modern age, new guidance is needed to address the needs of a global society. But it is up to each individual to find and investigate this guidance for themselves.

The solution to most problems begins by examining the past to determine how the problems began. A doctor begins a diagnosis by asking questions about a patient's health history and present symptoms. Only with a rational understanding of the background and acceptance of the present condition can we even begin to seek solutions to the world's problems.

The solution to big problems often requires new ways of thinking that must then be spread to others so old behaviors can be changed and a new culture established—a new civilization, perhaps, based on rational thinking, truthfulness, service to humanity and justice for all. Such a tremendous advance in the life of humanity cannot be achieved without the intelligent influence of a higher power. Fortunately, this is available to us because of the love of our Creator for all humanity.

> Bahá'u'lláh has proclaimed the promise of the oneness of humanity. Therefore, we must exercise the utmost love toward each other. We must be loving to all the people of the world. We must not consider any people the people of Satan, but know and recognize all as the servants of the one God. At most it is this: Some do not know; they must be guided and trained. They must be taught to love their fellow creatures and be encouraged in the acquisition of virtues. Some are ignorant; they must be informed. Some are as children, undeveloped; they must be helped to reach maturity. Some are ailing, their moral condition is unhealthy; they must be treated until their morals are purified. But the sick man is not to be hated because he is sick, the child must not

be shunned because he is a child, the ignorant one is not to be despised because he lacks knowledge. They must all be treated, educated, trained and assisted in love. Everything must be done in order that humanity may live under the shadow of God in the utmost security, enjoying happiness in its highest degree.[217]

217 'Abdu'l-Bahá, *The Promulgation of Universal Peace*, pp. 269-270.

Chapter 12:
Knowledge and Wisdom

As previously explained, rational thinking is a unique ability of the human realm. In contrast, irrational thinking, or thinking based on instinct rather than reasoning, distinguishes the animal realm from the human realm. Society often calls a person who speaks or acts irrationally an animal or animal-like. Why, then, do humans undervalue rational thinking when considering social and religious concepts and challenges?

Knowledge provides data upon which we can make sound judgements. Just *knowing* things may be interesting but not always useful. Wisdom involves applying a strong dose of perspective, insight and experience to put knowledge to use in a profound way. Knowledge is a part and wisdom is the whole.

Knowledge and wisdom have always been considered a great gift from God to man. Consider, for example, these passages from the Old Testament:

> **The heart of the prudent getteth knowledge; and the ear of the wise seeketh knowledge.**[218]

---

218 *Bible*, Proverbs 18: 15.

Through wisdom is an house builded; and by understanding it is established: And by knowledge shall the chambers be filled with all precious and pleasant riches. A wise man is strong; yea, a man of knowledge increaseth strength.[219]

And wisdom and knowledge shall be the stability of thy times, and strength of salvation: the fear of the Lord is his treasure.[220]

And they that be wise shall shine as the brightness of the firmament; and they that turn many to righteousness as the stars for ever and ever. But thou, O Daniel, shut up the words, and seal the book, even to the time of the end: many shall run to and fro, and knowledge shall be increased.[221]

My people are destroyed for lack of knowledge: because thou hast rejected knowledge, I will also reject thee, that thou shalt be no priest to me.[222]

Also consider passages in the New Testament from letters written by Paul to the early Christian churches. He advised that those who are ministers of God should be characterized by many good qualities, including "...By pureness, by knowledge..."[223]

Paul also counseled the early believers:

---

219 *Bible*, Proverbs 24: 3-5.

220 *Bible*, Isaiah 33: 6.

221 *Bible*, Daniel 12: 3-4.

222 *Bible*, Hosea 4:6

223 *Bible*, 2 Corinthians 6: 6.

That their hearts might be comforted, being knit together in love, and unto all riches of the full assurance of understanding, to the acknowledgement of the mystery of God, and of the Father, and of Christ; In whom are hid all the treasures of wisdom and knowledge. [224]

Two Types of Knowledge

There are two types of knowledge—acquired and innate. Acquired knowledge is attained primarily by the senses—sight, hearing, smell and touch. It springs from the desire to investigate and learn from the material world. Acquired knowledge is most often learned at school where we study other people's discoveries and strive to copy and build upon them. After completing our schooling, we are given a diploma to prove we have completed the curriculum. Our acquired knowledge is recognized and praised at every level of educational achievement from high school certificate to PhD.

Innate knowledge, on the other hand, distinguishes the Divine Educators Who by Their own admission had little or no opportunity for formal learning in schools. Without the help of formal education, however, Their knowledge far surpassed that of other humans in both material and spiritual topics.

...the pursuit of knowledge has been enjoined upon everyone, and knowledge itself is described by Bahá'u'lláh as "wings to man's life" and "a ladder for his ascent". Those whose high attainments in this respect make it possible for them to contribute in important ways to the advancement of civilization are deserving of society's recognition and gratitude. [225]

---

224 *Bible*, Colossians 2:3

225 Letter to an individual, The Universal House of Justice, Department of the Secretariat, March 14, 1996.

> The light of the people of the world is their knowledge and utterance...[226]

Awareness of things and concepts are of two kinds. First, there is awareness of the existence of things through our senses, such as sight, hearing, touch, smell and taste. But "knowing" things through our own minds is another kind that is often alluded to in the Scriptures:

> I have heard of thee by the hearing of the ear, but now mine eye seeth thee.[227]

> Blessed are the pure in heart, for they shall see God.[228]

> As long as I am in the world, I am the light of the world.[229]

> The signs and tokens of the Truth shine even as the midday sun, and yet the people are wandering, aimlessly and perplexedly, in the wilderness of ignorance and folly.[230]

> "Knowledge is a light which God casteth into the heart of whomsoever He willeth." It is this kind of knowledge which is and hath ever been praiseworthy, and not the limited knowledge that hath sprung forth from veiled and obscured minds.[231]

---

226 The Báb, *Selections from the Writings of the Báb*, p. 98.

227 *Bible*, Job 42: 5.

228 *Bible*, Mathew 5: 8.

229 *Bible*, John 9: 5.

230 Bahá'u'lláh, *The Kitab-i-Iqan,(Book of Certitude)*, p. 239

231 Bahá'u'lláh, *The Kitab-i-Iqa, (Book of Certitude)*, p. 46.

> The essence of all that We have revealed for thee is Justice, is for man to free himself from idle fancy and imitation, discern with the eye of oneness His glorious handiwork, and look into all things with a searching eye.[232]

Expanding on this final passage, the following qualities are required for us to think independently and determine what is true and appropriate for our time:

- We must strive to uphold justice in all of our ideas and actions.
- Our thoughts must be free from idle fancy or imaginings.
- Our actions should not blindly imitate outdated ideas and beliefs.
- We should attempt to see the "big picture" with the eye of oneness, that is to realize the interconnectedness of every aspect of humanity's life in this world.
- We should examine all issues independently with a searching eye.

When more people begin to think and act in this way, a greater maturity will become evident in all the affairs of humanity.

As previously discussed, the rational soul enables us to function in human society and establish common goals. Our focus is not so much on personal or private goals, when an individual's faith may play a stronger role. Within the larger context of human society, the element of faith is still needed. However, the importance of rational thinking seems to outweigh faith or feelings in order for humanity to take chances, move forward, and explore the unknown. Wisdom eventually emerges when we engage both the rational soul and faith, learning from experience how to predict the outcome of our decisions and actions. For humanity, this combination of reflecting

---

232 Bahá'u'lláh, *Tablets of Bahá'u'lláh*, p. 157.

on its history and patterns of empirical data along with faith creates a strong basis upon which to predict the future. As expressed by one of the Divine Educators:

> The past is the mirror of the future. Gaze ye therein and be apprised thereof; perchance ye may be aided thereby to recognize the Friend and may be not the cause of His displeasure. In this day the choicest fruit of the tree of knowledge is that which serveth the welfare of humanity and safeguardeth its interests.[233]

This quality of wisdom allows the Divine Educators to predict where and how humanity will suffer if the divine teachings are ignored. Humanity is in desperate need of such wisdom. How often have we heard about the short-sightedness of those who promote decisions based on their own advantage or desire, not foreseeing the future impact of such decisions on themselves as well as humanity? To achieve this treasured wisdom all decisions affecting the whole of humanity must be rational, reflecting a thoughtful evaluation of our common history and experiences. All decisions must also be founded on trust and faith in the fundamental unity of all humanity so that individuals will become inspired and develop the courage to move forward and develop ways to make the future safer and more productive for all.

The Divine Educators have always been praised for their ability to predict the future, earning them such titles as "Father" and "Divine Physician." They are able to detect the developing rational maturity of humanity and predict, in their wisdom, when humanity is moving forward. They inspire us with assurances of a glorious future if we continue along this path.

The Divine Educators often used words or phrases from our common vocabulary to try to describe for us the future of humanity.

---

233 Bahá'u'lláh, *The Tabernacle of Unity*, 1.16, p. 10

Many of these words have been misinterpreted or mistranslated, thereby coming to mean things that were never intended. As we've seen, the origins of words like heaven, paradise, hell, Satan, Devil, Angel or Divine help us to uncover the true meaning and true guidance intended by the Divine Educators in the Holy Scriptures. Even just these words, which are used in several Holy Scriptures, demonstrate the challenge of using common words to describe conditions or feelings that are not limited to this material world. Our human vocabulary is inadequate to this task, yet we strive to use everyday words to describe extra-ordinary experiences. For example, we say "My heart leaped when I saw my beloved," or "I am burning with jealousy." Through such common words and simple analogies, the Divine Educators strive to convey to us the profound concepts of spiritual qualities.

The Spirit of Faith and Immortality

Humans appear to be living in two worlds at the same time—this material world and another world of the spirit. Evidence of this second reality occurs while we are dreaming. In our dreams we seem to see, hear, touch and feel without the use of our physical senses. The Holy Scriptures refer to this reality as our spiritual reality, which far surpasses the importance of our physical reality. Consider the following description of the condition of this world today and how misled mankind has been:

> Alas! that humanity is completely submerged in imitations and unrealities notwithstanding the truth of divine religion has ever remained the same. Superstitions have obscured the fundamental reality, the world is darkened and the light of religion is not apparent. This darkness is conducive to differences and dissensions; rites and dogmas are many and various; therefore discord has arisen among the religious systems whereas religion is for the unification of mankind. True religion is the source

> of love and agreement amongst men, the cause of the development of praiseworthy qualities; but the people are holding to the counterfeit and imitation, negligent of the reality which unifies; so they are bereft and deprived of the radiance of religion.[234]

Bahá'u'lláh says the present world order is lamentably defective. Which constituency of the world order is *not* defective? How defective are the standards and constitutions of the world? Which parts are we to keep and which parts are we to throw away? How deeply do we have to go into the present order to find the defects within its structure?

Our physical reality is continually changing, going through periods of building up and tearing down, of progression and destruction. We are born, grow and become strong. We progress from childhood to youth to maturity. Gradually, we enter the stage of old age, and finally our body dies and decomposes, returning to the basic elements of the earth.

In contrast, according to many wisdom traditions including the Bahá'í Faith, our spiritual reality begins at the time of conception,[235] but it has no end. This spiritual reality, also called the rational soul, constantly progresses, both in this world and in worlds beyond this one. After physical death, the soul continues living in the spiritual world.

Just as a newborn is released from the tight confines of the womb when it is born into this world, so the soul experiences a release from the limitations of this world when it is born again into a world of the spirit. Science cannot yet explain the spirit that ignites a new being, which is certainly more than the beginning of a heartbeat or the first electrical impulse of a brain. It still cannot explain the transition of the soul—an entity we do not have instruments capable of detecting or measuring—into a spiritual world. Science cannot yet

---

234 'Abdu'l-Bahá, *The Promulgation of World Peace*.
235 Shoghi Effendi, *Lights of Guidance*.

define or measure the mind either. Therefore, the Divine Educators have extolled the concept of eternal life and exalted it above this material life. Indeed, they have explained that someone with no understanding of this spiritual reality and eternal life is like someone who is physically dead. The spirit of someone who has been awakened to the reality of eternal life, however, will never die, even though the physical life of the body will eventually end.

The Apostle Paul made the first and only mention of the spirit of faith in the New Testament:

> For we which live are always delivered unto death for Jesus' sake, that the life also of Jesus might be made manifest in our mortal flesh. So then death worketh in us, but life in you. We having the same spirit of faith, according as it is written, I believed, and therefore have I spoken; we also believe, and therefore speak...[236]

Further explanation about the 'spirit of faith' is given in the Holy Qur'án:

> You will never find a people who 'truly' believe in Alláh (God) and the Last Day loyal to those who defy Alláh (God) and His Messenger, even if they were their parents, children, siblings, or extended family. For those 'believers', Alláh (God) has instilled faith in their hearts and strengthened them with a spirit from Him.[237]

> They ask you 'O Prophet' about the spirit. Say, "Its nature is known only to my Lord, and you 'O humanity' have been given but little knowledge.[238]

---

236 *Bible*, 2 Corinthians 4:11-13
237 *Quran*, Al-Mujadila 58:22.
238 *Quran*, Al-Isra 17:85.

This spirit of faith will surely play a major role in humanity's development and understanding of the social needs of our time. Presently, our understanding of this important concept is in the stage of infancy, but with greater maturity humanity will surely increase its reliance on a strong spirit of faith to ensure the true unification of humanity.

> ... the human spirit, unless it be assisted by the spirit of faith, cannot become acquainted with the divine mysteries and the heavenly realities. It is like a mirror which, although clear, bright, and polished, is still in need of light. Not until a sunbeam falls upon it can it discover the divine mysteries.[239]

> The greatest power in the realm and range of human existence is spirit—the divine breath which animates and pervades all things... There is another Spirit, however, which may be termed the Divine, to which Jesus Christ refers when He declares that man must be born of its quickening and baptized with its living fire. Souls deprived of that Spirit are accounted as dead, though they are possessed of the human spirit. Jesus Christ has pronounced them dead inasmuch as they have no portion of the Divine Spirit. He says, "Let the dead bury their dead." In another instance, He declares, "That which is born of the flesh is flesh; and that which is born of the Spirit is spirit." By this He means that souls, though alive in the human kingdom, are nevertheless dead if devoid of this particular spirit of divine quickening. They have not partaken of the divine life of the higher Kingdom, for the soul which partakes of the power of the Divine Spirit is, verily, living.[240]

---

239 'Abdu'l-Bahá, *Some Answered Questions*, Part 4, Section 55, pp. 208-209.
240 'Abdu'l-Baha, *The Promulgation of Universal Peace*, pp. 58-59.

It is impossible to understand or describe the meaning of "spirit of faith" with common language since it is not of this material world. Words are not sufficient to describe this power, which is responsible for our recognition and love of the Divine. Evidence of this spirit of faith was witnessed amongst the early followers of every Divine Educator. Those who attained this spirit of faith became so detached from the material world that they forsook all thoughts of self and were prepared to sacrifice everything, even life itself, in order to awaken humanity to the new guidance revealed by the Divine Educator for that time.

The "Spirit of Faith," which the authors also call conscious faith to distinguish it from blind faith, seems to be a source of life, inspiration, eternal illumination and certitude that is given to humanity by the will and grace of the Divine and its intermediator, the Divine Educator.

> Seeing the possibilities and opportunities before them with new eyes, they witness firsthand the power of Divine assistance, as they strive to put into practice what they are learning and achieve results far exceeding their expectations. That the spirit of faith born out of intimate contact with the Word of God has such an effect on souls is by no means a new phenomenon.[241]

If "the reality of man is his thought, not his material body,"[242] then both happiness and sadness are reflections of a person's thoughts. In other words, to be in heaven or to be in hell are conditions of the spirit and not of the physical body. Even though we wish to understand everything based on our experiences in this physical life, we must expand our minds to grasp the meaning of higher concepts, such as "conditions of the spirit."

---

241 Universal House of Justice, December 27, 2005, letter to Conference of Continental Boards of Counsellors.

242 'Abdu'l-Bahá, *Paris Talks*, pp. 17-18.

With such expanded understanding, we can accept that heaven and hell are not physical places but rather conditions of a person's soul while living on Earth and preparing for life in the next world. Hell, then, is a word used to describe the condition of total selfishness, a search focused on his or her own personal salvation. On the other hand, heaven is a word used to describe a condition of total selflessness in which a person rationally understands the needs of humanity and becomes concerned for the well-being of all humankind.

We have been given the power of rational thought to guide our actions. Does it not make sense, then, to use our reasoning, strengthened by the courage inspired by the spirit of faith, to make wise plans for the future of humanity? Is it not clear that we are all responsible for our future, individually and collectively?

> The well-being of mankind, its peace and security, are unattainable unless and until its unity is firmly established. This unity can never be achieved so long as the counsels which the Pen of the Most High hath revealed are suffered to pass unheeded. Through the power of the words He hath uttered the whole of the human race can be illumined with the light of unity, and the remembrance of His Name is able to set on fire the hearts of all men, and burn away the veils that intervene between them and His glory.... Whoso ariseth, in this Day, to aid Our Cause, and summoneth to his assistance the hosts of a praiseworthy character and upright conduct, the influence flowing from such an action will, most certainly, be diffused throughout the whole world.[243]

---

243 Bahá'u'lláh, *Gleanings from the Writings of Bahá'u'lláh*, CXXXI, pp. 286-287.

The Need for Self-Evaluation

All our thoughts and actions make a difference in this world. Therefore, it is of vital importance to evaluate our own values and strive to eliminate any prejudices of race, nation, religion, political opinion, economic background or gender. All these prejudices are limiting factors that prevent true unity. Only independent investigation and education—not indoctrination—can overcome such deeply ingrained paradigms of thinking. Rational or reasonable solutions to humanity's problems cannot be achieved unless we abandon blind imitation of the past, including all harmful paradigms motivated by self-interest.

It is encouraging to note that humanity is making progress toward eliminating some of its long-standing prejudices such as sexism, nationalism, racism and ethnic bias, but unfortunately not religious prejudice.

> The enduring legacy of the twentieth century is that it compelled the peoples of the world to begin seeing themselves as the members of a single human race, and the earth as that race's common homeland. Despite the continuing conflict and violence that darken the horizon, prejudices that once seemed inherent in the nature of the human species are everywhere. Down with them come barriers that long divided the family of man.... That so fundamental a change could occur in so brief a period—virtually overnight in the perspective of historical time—suggests the magnitude of the possibilities for the future.
>
> Tragically, organized religion, whose very reason for being entails service to the cause of brotherhood and peace, behaves all too frequently as one of the most formidable obstacles in the path; to cite a particular painful fact, it has long lent its credibility to fanaticism....

The issue comes sharply into focus when one considers what has been achieved elsewhere. In the past, apart from isolated exceptions, women were regarded as an inferior breed, their nature hedged about by superstitions, denied the opportunity to express the potentialities of the human spirit and relegated to the role of serving the needs of men. Clearly, there are many societies where such conditions persist and are even fanatically defended. At the level of global discourse, however, the concept of the equality of the sexes has, for all practical purposes, now assumed the force of universally accepted principle. It enjoys similar authority in most of the academic community and information media. So basic has been the revisioning that exponents of male supremacy must look for support on the margins of responsible opinion.

The beleaguered battalions of nationalism face a similar fate. With each passing crisis in world affairs, it becomes easier for the citizen to distinguish between a love of country that enriches one's life, and submission to inflammatory rhetoric designed to provoke hatred and fear of others. Even where it is expedient to participate in the familiar nationalistic rites, public response is as often marked by feelings of awkwardness as it is by the strong convictions and ready enthusiasm of earlier times. The effect has been reinforced by the restructuring steadily taking place in the international order. Whatever the shortcomings of the United Nations system in its present form, and however handicapped its ability to take collective military action against aggression, no one can mistake the fact that the fetish of absolute national sovereignty is on its way to extinction.

Racial and ethnic prejudices have been subjected to equally summary treatment by historical processes that have little patience left for such pretensions. Here, rejection of the past has been especially decisive. Racism is now tainted by its association with the horrors of the twentieth century to the degree that it has taken on something of the character of a spiritual disease. While surviving as a social attitude in many parts of the world— and as a blight on the lives of a significant segment of humankind—racial prejudice has become so universally condemned in principle that no body of people can any longer safely allow themselves to be identified with it.

It is not that a dark past has been erased and a new world of light has suddenly been born. Vast numbers of people continue to endure the effects of ingrained prejudices of ethnicity, gender, nation, caste and class. All the evidence indicates that such injustices will long persist as the institutions and standards that humanity is devising only slowly become empowered to construct a new order of relationships and to bring relief to the oppressed. The point, rather, is that a threshold has been crossed from which there is no credible possibility of return. Fundamental principles have been identified, articulated, accorded broad publicity and are becoming progressively incarnated in institutions capable of imposing them on public behaviour. There is no doubt that, however protracted and painful the struggle, the outcome will be to revolutionize relationships among all peoples, at the grassroots level.

As the twentieth century opened, the prejudice that seemed more likely than any other to succumb to the forces of change was that of religion.... With every day that passes, danger grows that the rising fires of religious prejudice will ignite a worldwide conflagration the consequences of which are unthinkable. Such a danger civil government, unaided, cannot overcome. Nor should we delude ourselves that appeals for mutual tolerance can alone hope to extinguish animosities that claim to possess Divine sanction. The crisis calls on religious leadership for a break with the past as decisive as those that opened the way for society to address equally corrosive prejudices of race, gender and nation. Whatever justification exists for exercising influence in matters of conscience lies in serving the well-being of humankind. At this greatest turning point in the history of civilization, the demands of such service could not be more clear. "The well-being of mankind, its peace and security, are unattainable", Bahá'u'lláh urges, "unless and until its unity is firmly established.[244]

---

244 The Universal House of Justice, *Letter to the World's Religious Leaders*, April 2002.

Chapter 13:
Why We Need Conscious Faith

What Is Conscious Faith?

Immanuel Kant, a well-known 18th century German philosopher, proposed that a new religion must sometimes be created when an old religion is clearly no longer logical or reasonable. The New Testament states that "...*new wine must be put into new bottles...*,"[245] an analogy that suggests today's rational thinkers, unsatisfied with many old teachings that are not rational, require new religious teachings. Both viewpoints define the basic concept of progressive revelation, a course correction along with expanded information provided successively by Divine Educators.

We have defined a person's true reality as their thoughts, which generate conscious knowledge—being aware of our knowledge of certain things. But thoughts can also generate conscious faith, which may seem to contradict earlier statements. Isn't faith the flip side of knowledge... a belief in something that can't be proven?

Not always.

Belief in something that can't be proven or simply imitates past traditions is generally called "blind faith." But there is another kind of faith that is based on a conscious search for reality using all our

---

245 *Bible*, Luke 5:38

human faculties, including rational thought, but is kindled by the "Spirit of Faith" as described earlier. The authors call this "conscious faith." Some may call it insight, intuition or epiphany."

Conscious faith is not dependent on our efforts or success at seeking information. It seems to come from an unknown place, called the spiritual world by some, and often reveals to us a previously unknown path to resolve a problem. This perception becomes particularly important when our thoughts compel us to take certain actions to achieve an outcome we have envisioned. Conscious faith, like conscious knowledge, is unique to the human realm.

The life of a seed demonstrates the development of conscious faith. As mentioned earlier, a seed has the potential to become a mighty tree if it is provided with good soil, abundant sunshine and plentiful water. Like the seed, conscious faith also requires favorable growing conditions—a desire to study and learn the divine teachings, development of personal virtues, detachment from material possessions, an attitude of sacrificial service to others and selfless humility based on recognition of the unlimited knowledge of the Creator. When such conditions are nurtured, the seed of conscious faith can grow into a mighty tree.

How can we know whether conscious faith is divinely inspired or based on the "vain imaginings" of humans? If every thorn would claim to be a beautiful flower, and every deceptive man would call himself a divinely inspired soul, then what is the test?

To determine if a religious leader or a person of faith is speaking truth, consider the ultimate goal of that person. Is the speaker's motivation selfish or selfless? Are we deceived by appearances? Too often we value the ideas of a person based on how much we admire them, or the abundance of their material possessions, or the amount of money they are asking us to invest or spend with them. Evaluating the lives of the Divine Educators, such as Jesus, shows that Their most valued ideas and possessions are the words of guidance They proclaim, for Their words are divinely-inspired.

Another test is to examine the degree of sacrifice made by those who proclaim new ideas. Unlike mere philosophers, the Divine Educators are prepared to offer every possession, even their lives, to share guidance with humanity. The Divine Educators possess the gifts of conscious knowledge and conscious faith. They could have lived in relative comfort but consciously accepted a life of suffering, always putting the well-being of humanity before their own needs. The Divine Educators demonstrate great wisdom and insight into the future of humanity. They perceive the difficulties afflicting humanity and prescribe the cure. They also perceive humanity's shortcomings and give strong warnings about what may happen if people continue to turn away from divinely inspired guidance.

Today, we have entered a new time of technology and communication. Even though we have achieved great material and intellectual advancement, humanity's spiritual development is lagging. Are we not living in the time prophesied by Paul in this passage from the New Testament?

> This know also, that in the last days perilous times shall come. For men shall be lovers of their own selves, covetous, boasters, proud, blasphemers, disobedient to parents, unthankful, unholy, without natural affection, trucebreakers, false accusers, incontinent, fierce, despisers of those that are good, traitors, heady, high-minded, lovers of pleasures more than lovers of God; having a form of godliness but denying the power thereof: from such turn away.[246]

The world's religions may include many practices and beliefs that we may find difficult to accept. Such practices may even conflict with rational thinking, particularly when conscious knowledge defines our faith and our desire to promote the well-being of all humanity.

---

246 *Bible*, 2 Timothy 3: 1-6

> In passages that draw not only on the Qur'án, but with equal facility and insight on the Old and New Testaments, the Messengers of God are depicted as agents of a single, unbroken process, the awakening of the human race to its spiritual and moral potentialities. A humanity which has come of age can respond to a directness of teaching that goes beyond the language of parable and allegory; faith is a matter not of blind belief, but of conscious knowledge. Nor is the guidance of an ecclesiastical elite any longer required: the gift of reason confers on each individual in this new age of enlightenment and education the capacity to respond to Divine guidance.[247]

The Divine Educators all claim to receive Their light or knowledge from the same Source, yet it is not possible to adequately identify this Source or even explain how these Teachers have acquired what appears to be innate or inborn knowledge. Somehow, without tutoring or independent research, They possess the capacity to understand abstract concepts, such as the reality of life after death, and the differences between this material world and the next world.

Even though all of the Divine Educators have had this gift of innate knowledge from childhood, many have described a particular moment when it became clear that They were blessed to bring the latest divine guidance to humanity.

Recall the story of Abraham when He bravely followed God's command to sacrifice His son (Genesis 22); the experiences of Moses when a voice spoke to Him from a burning bush (Exodus 3); Jesus when the Holy Spirit descended upon Him like a dove (Mark 1:10, Luke 3:22, John 1:32; Muhammad, who was illiterate before the angel Gabriel commanded Him to read by saying "Recite"; and, most recently, Bahá'u'lláh when an angel (the Maid of) appeared to Him

---

247 Bahá'í International Community, "A Statement on Bahá'u'lláh."

in prison promising that God would make Him victorious by His pen. All these Divine Educators have claimed that Their knowledge is not from Themselves but from a higher Source that has compelled Them to proclaim this knowledge as laws and guidance for the well-being of humanity.

Each of the Divine Educators also promised the coming of another Divine Educator in the future, calling Him by different titles, such as the Messiah, the Anointed One, the Spirit of truth and the Promised One. For example, Christ told His disciples...

> I have yet many things to say unto you, but ye cannot bear them now. Howbeit when he, the Spirit of truth, is come, he will guide you into all truth: for he shall not speak of himself; but whatsoever he shall hear, that shall he speak: and he will shew you things to come[248]

> Beware of false prophets, which come to you in sheep's clothing but inwardly they are ravening wolves. Ye shall know them by their fruits. Do men gather grapes of thorns or figs of thistles? Even so every good tree bringeth forth good fruit; but a corrupt tree bringeth forth evil fruit.[249]

Divine Educators each release a new surge of spiritual power into the world, energizing the process of renewal and progress that comes with Their new divine revelation.

> ...the Word of God, and all the potentialities thereof, shall be manifested unto men in strict conformity with such conditions as have been foreordained by Him Who is the All-Knowing, the All-Wise.... Should the

---

248 *Bible*, John 16: 12-13.
249 *Bible*, Matthew 7:15-17.

> Word be allowed to release suddenly all the energies latent within it, no man could sustain the weight of so mighty a Revelation.[250]

Every Divine Educator has given predictions about the future of humanity as well as warnings for the consequences of failing to heed those warnings. In many Scriptures, future Divine Educators are referred to with the words "I will return" as though their return will be the coming of new knowledge and not necessarily the decomposed return of their body. In fact, we have no knowledge of what the past Divine Teachers such as Moses and Jesus and Muhammad looked like, so how would we even recognize them based on bodily resurrection? As a result of Their guidance, the social order of humanity will surge forward at an accelerated rate until humanity will enter a stage of decline when people again begin to neglect and corrupt the guidance of the past.

For centuries, human knowledge has continued to reflect the light or wisdom revealed by the Divine Educators. Each individual, we have been told, has the capacity to study the guidance of the Divine Educators, and this guidance will then have a great influence on the development of the human soul. To imagine that this spiritual development is the result of an individual's own effort alone without such divine guidance is unreasonable. Consider the counsel that Jesus gave to His disciples as they began to go out and share His guidance with the world:

> And he said unto them, Take nothing for your journey, ... neither bread, neither money; neither have two coats apiece. And whatsoever house ye enter into, there abide, and thence depart. And whosoever will not receive you, when ye go out of that city, shake off the very dust from your feet for a testimony against them.[251]

---

250 Bahá'u'lláh, quoted in Shoghi Effendi, *The Promised Day Is Come*, p. 118.
251 *Bible*, Luke 9: 3-5.

This statement suggests that the disciples should trust that their needs will be met while they share the guidance of God with others. Neither should they be upset if they are rejected by others. The divine teachings are for everyone and should be given and received with no thought of material gain.

A Rational Reason to Believe

Conscious faith is a belief in something that does not have direct evidence to prove it is true, but has enough circumstantial evidence or deductive logic for one to say it is true or most likely true. It requires a rational reason to gain our belief.

In American criminal court, a guilty verdict must be supported by unbiased evidence that establishes proof of guilt "beyond a reasonable doubt." This is a very high standard. In American civil court, however, the standard is a bit lower, requiring only a "preponderance of evidence" to prove something is true. In other words, there must be a greater than 50 percent chance that the claim is true, which means a degree of doubt can co-exist. The legal system considers this to be rational thinking in a civil proceeding.

Deductive logic falls into the "preponderance" standard. Since the sun has risen every morning since you were born, it is fair to conclude that the sun will rise tomorrow morning, though you cannot prove that the world will not end before then. This belief passes the "preponderance" standard and seems like a reasonable deductive conclusion. You have conscious faith in the rising of the sun.

In religion, many topics and claims rely on conscious faith. Not blind faith, which requires no rational basis, but faith based on reasonable arguments and enough circumstantial evidence to be convincing. Belief in life after death qualifies for some as blind faith—"blind" because they have not investigated the claim and only believed what they were told—and "conscious" faith for others who have done their due diligence. There is always room for honest debate among those who have conscious faith in something, but there can be no honest debate when people have forfeited reason for blind faith because they have no evidence and no arguments to debate.

As in philosophy, many of the arguments presented by various wisdom traditions in favor of certain principles are logical in nature and require only one thing from the individual who wishes to investigate—not a belief in a Higher Power, as one might expect, but simply a commitment to study the evidence and reach a logical conclusion like any good juror.

Chapter 14:
An Ever-Advancing Civilization

Years ago, anthropologist Margaret Mead was asked by a student what she considered to be the first sign of civilization in a culture. The student expected Mead to talk about fishhooks or clay pots or grinding stones. Mead said… the first sign of civilization in an ancient culture was a femur (thighbone) that had been broken and then healed. Mead explained that in the animal kingdom, if you break your leg, you die. You cannot run from danger, get to the river for a drink or hunt for food. You are meat for prowling beasts. No animal survives a broken leg long enough for the bone to heal. A broken femur that has healed is evidence that someone has taken time to stay with the one who fell, has bound up the wound, has carried the person to safety and has tended the person through recovery. Helping someone else through difficulty is where civilization starts. Mead said, "We become our best when we serve others."[252]

---

252 Ira Byock, Qura website, April 4, 2022.

A Continuous but Cyclical Process

So, what is civilization exactly? A formal definition is that civilization is the "stage of human social and cultural development and organization that is considered most advanced." Human advancement can be assessed in many areas including technology and discoveries. The most important advancement is probably maturation of human behavior.

> All men have been created to carry forward an ever-advancing civilization. The Almighty beareth Me witness: To act like the beasts of the field is unworthy of man. Those virtues that befit his dignity are forbearance, mercy, compassion and loving-kindness towards all the peoples and kindreds of the earth.[253]

When this stage of development is attained, prejudices of all kinds are eliminated, humanity is regarded as one human family and Earth as one common homeland. Everybody will contribute their share toward this ever-advancing civilization, one in which all the arts and sciences promote in various ways the unity, well-being, security and peace of all humankind.

Civilization progresses in a continuous but cyclical process of crisis and victory. Out of the turmoil and disorder of a society in decline, a new civilization emerges in various places soon after the coming of a Divine Educator. New teachings contribute to a fundamental unity of thought that fosters rapid development of new concepts and discoveries. With each cycle, humanity increases its capacity to rationally solve ever more complex problems. In our lifetimes, we have seen many profound changes, but much greater progress was predicted by 'Abdu'l-Bahá over a hundred years ago:

---

253 Bahá'u'lláh, *Gleanings from the Writings of Bahá'u'lláh*, CIX, p. 215.

No matter how far the material world advances, it cannot establish the happiness of mankind. Only when material and spiritual civilization are linked and coordinated will happiness be assured. Then material civilization will not contribute its energies to the forces of evil in destroying the oneness of humanity, for in material civilization good and evil advance together and maintain the same pace. For example, consider the material progress of man.... Schools and colleges, hospitals, philanthropic institutions, scientific academies and temples of philosophy have been founded, but hand in hand with these evidences of development, the invention and production of means and weapons for human destruction have correspondingly increased....

All this is the outcome of material civilization; therefore, although material advancement furthers good purposes in life, at the same time it serves evil ends. The divine civilization is good because it cultivates morals. Consider what the Prophets of God have contributed to human morality. Jesus Christ summoned all to the Most Great Peace through the acquisition of pure morals. If the moral precepts and foundations of divine civilization become united with the material advancement of man, there is no doubt that the happiness of the human world will be attained and that from every direction the glad tidings of peace upon earth will be announced. Then humankind will achieve extraordinary progress, the sphere of human intelligence will be immeasurably enlarged, wonderful inventions will appear, and the spirit of God will reveal itself; all men will consort in joy and fragrance, and eternal life will be conferred upon the children of the Kingdom.[254]

---

254 'Abdu'l-Bahá, *The Promulgation of Universal Peace*, pp. 109-110.

Great advancements in civilization cannot take place unless they are supported by the divine guidance that directs and protects humanity. For example, when a scientific discovery like nuclear energy is used to benefit humanity, it can be a great source of good. But if its use is not guided by Divine Teachings, it can cause the destruction of human life and Earth's environment.

There is now an urgent need for unity of thought on global issues affecting humanity. Our collective future depends on the united efforts of all nations. Some four hundred years ago, the English poet John Donne wrote, "No man is an island, entire of itself. ... Any man's death diminishes me because I am involved in mankind..." The same can now be said of each nation when considering our planet. No nation can stand alone; all need to work together for the common good.

> Let your vision be world-embracing, rather than confined to your own self. ... It is incumbent upon every man, in this Day, to hold fast unto whatsoever will promote the interests, and exalt the station, of all nations and just governments. ...Whatsoever hath led the children of men to shun one another, and hath caused dissensions and divisions amongst them, hath, through the revelation of these words, been nullified and abolished. ... Of old it hath been revealed: "Love of one's country is an element of the Faith of God.".... however, in (this) day...: "It is not his to boast who loveth his country, but it is his who loveth the world."[255]

Globalization must be the goal of our emerging world-wide society. A new global civilization is evolving that embraces the best of previous cultures but is uniquely suited to the needs of today. Divine guidance with a global perspective is a requirement for this next stage of a global civilization based on service to humanity, a

---

255 Bahá'u'lláh, *Gleanings from the Writings of Bahá'u'lláh*, LXIII, pp. 94-95.

stage that will ensure the preservation, health and well-being of all forms of life on Earth.

> Globalization itself is an intrinsic feature of the evolution of human society. It has brought into existence a socio-economic culture that, at the practical level, constitutes the world in which the aspirations of the human race will be pursued in the century .... No objective observer, if he is fair-minded in his judgement, will deny that both of the two contradictory reactions it is arousing are, in large measure, well justified. The unification of human society, forged by the fires of the twentieth century, is a reality that with every passing day opens breathtaking new possibilities. A reality also being forced on serious minds everywhere, is the claim of justice to be the one means capable of harnessing these great potentialities to the advancement of civilization. It no longer requires the gift of prophecy to realize that the fate of humanity ... will be determined by the relationship established between these two fundamental forces of the historical process, the inseparable principles of unity and justice.[256]

Future Society

How amazing that we can now access knowledge of the past and the present, as well as predictions for the future, with just a few clicks of a finger on a laptop or mobile phone. Is this not advancement of our civilization? Those who pursue knowledge so easily can no longer be satisfied with the blind faith of our ancestors. Future generations will require even more logical and rational explanations of religion, politics and social issues and will resist complying with old paradigms. Even the Holy Scriptures must be informed by science analyzed by

---

256 *Century of Light*, prepared under the supervision of the Universal House of Justice, p. 128.

rational thinking. The need for divine assistance has never been more needed.

A new Divine Educator Who came nearly two hundred years ago proclaimed that humanity was now entering the time of maturity when rational thinking and conscious knowledge must be combined with conscious faith. The teachings of Bahá'u'lláh (1817-1892), the founder of the Bahá'í Faith, are already well-established around the world. Millions of people have found these teachings to be the most logical and rational foundation for a new concept of religion. The Bahá'í Faith provides explanations for the prophecies and teachings of the past and is introducing a new pattern of life based on service to humanity. Bright prospects for the future of humanity inspire those who strive to follow these Teachings in their own lives.

> Unlike the Dispensations of the past, the Revelation of God to this age has given birth, to "a living organism", whose laws and institutions constitute "the essentials of a Divine Economy", "a pattern for future society", and "the one agency for the unification of the world, and the proclamation of the reign of righteousness and justice upon the earth.[257]

As old ways of thinking decline and fade, a new generation armed with rational thinking is beginning to mold the shape of future society. Their thinking may be advanced, but if they are not guided by divine teachings they will continue to be confronted with life-threatening conflicts and difficulties in this world. Reliance on computers and other forms of artificial intelligence may improve our access to timely information and hopefully ensure that the next generation does not fall into the ignorance of blind faith.

---

257 *Century of Light*, prepared under the supervision of the Universal House of Justice.

These words, written during the height of World War II, encourage the youth of today to take on the responsibilities of the future of humanity:

> Upon the present generation of youth will devolve the weighty task of helping to construct a new world after the effects of this tragic war have passed away. They must be ever conscious of their supreme duty towards their fellow-men - the duty of holding up to their enquiring gaze the model upon which a sound future society can be constructed. This is the system of Bahá'u'lláh which the Bahá'ís must first learn themselves to live up to, and then share with the whole world.
>
> Unlike the Dispensation of Christ, unlike the Dispensation of Muhammad, unlike all the Dispensations of the past, the apostles of Bahá'u'lláh in every land, wherever they labor and toil, have before them in clear, in unequivocal and emphatic language, all the laws, the regulations, the principles, the institutions, the guidance, they require for the prosecution and consummation of their task. ... Therein lies the distinguishing feature of the Bahá'í Revelation. Therein lies the strength of the unity of the Faith, of the validity of a Revelation that claims not to destroy or belittle previous Revelations, but to connect, unify, and fulfill them...[258]

The Advent of Social Justice

Humanity has long been challenged to establish universal standards for justice, particularly in defining basic human rights. More than twenty-five hundred years ago, the first Declaration of Human Rights, today called the Cyrus Cylinder, was proclaimed by Persian

---

258 Shoghi Effendi, *Dawn of a New Day*, p. 180.

Emperor Cyrus the Great. Among the many freedoms granted in this Declaration were the right to choose one's own religion and the establishment of racial equality. In every age and place, humanity has continued to struggle with questions of justice. A civilization cannot be ever advancing if it does not address social justice.

How can we determine the future outcome of present social movements and judge whether such movements promote justice or not? What appears to be justice for some people today may eventually be considered an injustice to some or all of a population. While history is full of many such examples, today we can cite severe abuses of human rights in many locations around the world.

In our search for justice, constant vigilance is needed to overcome prejudices and fanaticism and to strengthen rational thinking as opposed to irrational faith.

> The best beloved of all things in My sight is Justice; turn not away therefrom if thou desirest Me, and neglect it not that I may confide in thee. By its aid thou shalt see with thine own eyes and not through the eyes of others, and shalt know of thine own knowledge and not through the knowledge of thy neighbor. Ponder this in thy heart; how it behooveth thee to be. Verily justice is My gift to thee and the sign of My loving-kindness. Set it then before thine eyes.[259]

Whenever a Divine Educator proclaims new teachings, history demonstrates the emergence of a pattern of social justice and the blossoming of a new civilization followed, unfortunately, by a period of decline as people gradually turn away from the divine guidance. A good example is the rise and fall of the Roman Empire. With the coming of Jesus and the teachings of Christianity, a new civilization arose in Greece, Rome and Europe, with new discoveries, inventions and expansion of thought. The former barbaric and materialistic

---

259 Bahá'u'lláh, *The Hidden Words of Bahá'u'lláh*, from the Arabic, Number 2.

societies were gradually infused with the spiritual teachings of Jesus, causing a change in thinking throughout the whole region.

A similar transformation was witnessed with the coming of Muhammad amongst the people of Arabia some six hundred years after Christ. These nomadic people were brought out of the darkness of ignorance to establish a civilization renowned for its excellence in medicine, architecture, mathematics and physics.

Now, however, a period of great decline has occurred because people have turned away from the divine teachings of all Scriptures.

Today, the critical bond between God and humanity is being stretched to its breaking point. Social justice is hard to find, if it exists at all. If this trend continues, humanity will again decline to a state of desperation. It will be a time of great distress as foretold centuries ago:

> **For then shall be great tribulation, such as was not since the beginning of the world to this time, no, nor ever shall be.**[260]

Submission and Obedience

All kinds of organizations and social movements, whether based on religious, political, or other allegiances, require a certain degree of submission and obedience. Generally, the difference between submission and obedience can be difficult to discern.

The authors use the term submission to imply a certain degree of blind faith or blind adherence to obscure or unknown principles. Submission does not require the individual to rationally evaluate why or how an idea or action is performed, simply to perform it as prescribed. A person's decision to accept this path is usually based on emotions and traditions rather than facts.

As an example, a recent speech by an Islamic cleric on YouTube instructed Muslims not to question their faith, but to be content and

---

260 *Bible*, Mathew 24: 21.

submissive to the decisions of their ancestors, who suffered to bring the teachings of Islam to their country. Although submission may be standard for religious, political and social movements, it establishes value for ignorance, which contradicts rational thinking. In many cases, a group's standards or rules requiring total submission contain ideas or propose actions that are not reasonable or logical.

When submission is the foundation of one's beliefs and actions, the individual may easily deny their own responsibility and maintain that all responsibility is with the person or group that sets the standard and requires submission. In some instances, submission to a set of rules or beliefs is explained as one's fate or destiny, thus the individual cannot be held accountable or blameworthy for their actions. Such standards can often lead to disunity and separation between individuals.

Obedience, in the authors' usage, is different. One should not obey spiritual laws and teachings out of fear of punishment for disobedience but rather out of love for the Divine Educator.

> **Walk in My statutes for love of Me and deny thyself that which thou desirest if thou seekest My pleasure.**[261]

A second reason to obey spiritual laws is out of love for society and for the safety, well-being and unity of all people. Spiritual principles exist to help us make a more advanced society possible. This kind of compliance is totally consistent with rational thinking. When we agree to obey certain rules or meet certain standards, we work hard to do that because we have previously agreed with the rules or standards based on our previous investigation. In some cases, we agree to obey certain laws even if we do not fully agree with or understand them. We agree not out of blind faith but because we have been put to the test so much that we sometimes must agree we still don't know everything.

---

261 Bahá'u'lláh, *The Hidden Words of Bahá'u'lláh.*

In driving from one city to another, we agree to obey stated guidelines, rules and steps, all of which we agree are important for a safe journey, even though we might disagree with specific speed limits. We buckle our seatbelts, drive on the correct side of the road, brake for stoplights when no other cars are present and basically follow all rules for driving. Obedience to these rules is essential for our own safety as well as the safety of others. When decisions are based on rational thinking, obedience to known rules and standards is logical to achieve our goals. Disobeying puts our goals at risk.

The rational soul of all people provides the ability and responsibility to engage all their powers to search, question, and evaluate all sources of knowledge before making well-informed decisions. Once decisions have been made, everyone must commit to obediently follow the rules and steps required and take responsibility for their actions. Decisions cannot be based solely on emotions or illogical beliefs. The search for knowledge and truth is an obligation for every individual in this complex and confusing time. When humanity increases its reliance on rational thinking in every aspect of its shared social life, we will finally attain to the highest level of human existence.

We must overcome ignorance, embrace rationality and dedicate ourselves to the search for truth wherever it may take us. Truth must be based on knowledge and reason, and it must be the basis for the education of every child and adult.

Summary of Main Conclusions

The Soul of Humanity is a general appeal to abandon blind faith and apply rational thinking to all important matters of life from science and relationships to politics and religion.

One God

The Soul of Humanity attempts to build a rational case for the existence of a single God, an indescribable force responsible for the existence of the natural world. It also offers evidence that each human has a rational soul, and that this soul connects humans to a spiritual world that perhaps cannot yet be measured scientifically because we neither have adequate instrumentation nor the knowledge of what to measure.

One Unfolding Religion

The Soul of Humanity presents a rational explanation for the sequential appearance of "Prophets" and their Teachings, which have provided the spiritual and ethical foundation for the world's great wisdom traditions often referred to as "religions." According to this book's explanation, these successive wisdom traditions revealed a progressive unfolding of spiritual truths and practical laws, each "Revelation" building on the knowledge developed by its predecessors. In other words, there is only one religion of God that humankind is discovering incrementally in the same way that we are discovering the laws and principles of science over time.

If there is one God known by dissimilar names and understood differently by diverse people, and if there is just one religion that has been revealed in stages but unfortunately corrupted and misinterpreted to serve the selfish interests of humans, where does that leave us? *The Soul of Humanity* proposes that by expanding our spiritual knowledge and modernizing many of the old material laws, each "Prophet" has provided humanity with an updated owner's manual for living well in an ever-advancing society and getting along with others. All we have to do is consult that manual and follow its advice.

Unfortunately, humans usually favor the "Prophet" they already know and persecute those who announce changes. People have such affection for their accepted Prophet they ignore all the previous Prophets and condemn any who follow. Refusing to even consider the claims of a new Divine Educator may seem irrational and short-sighted, but this is how devout belief becomes prejudice. And yet we find that each of the founders of the major wisdom traditions acknowledged their continuous chain of custody of truth. According to Gautama Buddha:

> I am not the first Buddha who came upon the earth nor shall I be the last. In due time another Buddha will arise in the world, a holy one, a supremely enlightened one, endowed with wisdom in conduct, auspicious, knowing the universe, an incomparable leader of men, a master of angels and mortals. He will reveal to you the same eternal truths, which I have taught you. He will preach his religion, glorious in its origin, glorious at the climax and glorious at the goal. He will proclaim a religious life, wholly perfect and pure such as I now proclaim. His disciples will number many thousands while mine number many hundreds.[262]

---

262 Gautama Buddha, *Gospel of Buddha by Carus* (Ceylon Sources), pp. 217-218

According to the Bahá'i Writings:

> Every prophet predicted the coming of a successor and every successor acknowledged the Truth of the predecessor. Moses prophesied the coming of Christ. Christ acknowledged Moses. His Highness Christ foretold the appearance of Muhammad, and Muhammad accepted The Christ and Moses. When all these divine prophets were united with each other, why should we disagree?[263]

Nevertheless, many people wonder how there can be a unity of religions when they have conflicting laws. But a deeper look into the fundamental verities proposed by each wisdom tradition shows they are of two types: spiritual laws and practical or material laws.

> The spiritual part never changes. All the Manifestations of God and His Prophets have taught the same truths and given the same spiritual law. They all teach the one code of morality... The practical part of religion deals with exterior forms and ceremonies, and with modes of punishment for certain offences...[264]

> In the time of Moses, there were ten crimes punishable by death. When Christ came this was changed; the old axiom "an eye for an eye, and a tooth for a tooth" was converted into "Love your enemies, do good to them that hate you," the stern old law being changed into one of love, mercy and forbearance! In the former days the punishment for theft was the cutting off of the right hand; in our time this law could not be so applied. In this age, a man who curses his father is allowed to

---

263 US Bahá'í News Service, "Star of the West: Excerpts #2," October 1911–February 1913

264 'Abdu'l-Bahá, *Paris Talks*.

> live, when formerly he would have been put to death. It is therefore evident that whilst the spiritual law never alters, the practical rules must change their application with the necessities of the time.[265]

One Human Family

The Soul of Humanity suggests that a fundamental teaching of all existing wisdom traditions—strongly inferred by the older ones and made abundantly clear in the most recent teachings—is that every individual is a member of one magnificently diverse human family. This oneness of all humanity transcends differences of culture, class, ethnicity, race, customs, opinions or temperaments.

> Ye are the fruits of one tree, and the leaves of one branch. Deal ye with one another with the utmost love and harmony, with friendliness and fellowship.[266]

Rationality and Prejudice

The Soul of Humanity proposes a number of other conclusions that the authors attempt to justify through rational thinking.

- Rational thinking usually reaches incorrect conclusions when the information analyzed is incomplete, purposely or inadvertently distorted, misunderstood or otherwise flawed. Trusted sources sometimes prove to be untrustworthy. It is up to each individual to seek the most trustworthy information available at the time and do their own rational analysis.

- Science and religion are not competing knowledge systems. Since both are the creation of one God, they must be in harmony with each other. Apparent differences are due to incomplete

---

265 'Abdu'l-Bahá, *Paris Talks.*
266 Bahá'u'lláh, *Gleanings from the Writings of Bahá'u'lláh.*

knowledge of one or the other or misunderstandings derived from false information or unproven theories, even those that are generally accepted.

- Regrettably, religion has often been the cause of disunity and strife, not because the original Teachings were flawed but because they have been so often misinterpreted, hijacked for selfish purposes, tainted by innate human prejudices, and corrupted in countless other ways.

- The lack of universal education, particularly the withholding of education for women and girls in many parts of the world, has contributed to a global society that lacks the knowledge and critical thinking skills needed for solving the world's problems. When education devolves into indoctrination that discourages independent thinking, however, the danger escalates.

- Prejudices, often rooted in blind faith and adherence to meaningless traditions and outdated rituals, is a frequent companion of ignorance. For civilization to advance, all prejudices must be annihilated, including racism, sexism, ageism, cultural and ethnical stereotypes, language and religious biases.

Social Transformation

The three onenesses—one God, one unfolding religion, one human family—are the foundation on which is built a remarkable and rational system for bringing about meaningful social transformation and addressing the frustrating problems faced by humanity today. Exploring this system rationally is the mission of the next book in this series, *Humanity Coming of Age*, due in 2024.

Research and Study Sources

For those who want to consult the sacred Writings of the wisdom traditions discussed in this book, we recommend the following sources:

Bahá'í Library (Online)

The definitive online library of authoritative Bahai Writtings and book/papers about the Bahai Faith. Many are available for reading or downloading in multiple formats such as PDF, DOCX and HTML

https://bahai-library.com/Writings

Uplifting Words (Online)

An online list of Bahá'í-only texts in multiple formats for reading or download.

https://www.upliftingwords.org/post/baha-i-sacred-texts

Ocean 2.0 Interfaith Reader

An immersive library of the world's sacred literature. Read or listen to texts from these religions: Hindu, Judaism, Confucian, Tao, Islam, Zoroastrianism, Jainism, Buddhist, Christian, Bahai Faith.

https://sacred-traditions.org/ocean/

Acknowledgements

We must first acknowledge all of the world's great wisdom traditions and those who for millennia have labored to recover, preserve and translate the collective knowledge of the Divine Educators in a form accessible to all humanity. Thanks also to the many advisors and readers of the manuscript who have helped immensely to improve the content and clarity of our prose.

Thanks also to our publishing company, Calumet Editions, and its talented staff—Ian Graham Leask, publisher and substantive editor, and Rick Polad, copyeditor—for their commitment and long hours correcting our mistakes, improving our language and style, and making sure that our book on rational thinking had no (or few) lapses in logic. The authors appreciate every challenge they gave us.

About the Authors

Massoud Kazemzadeh, PhD

Dr. Kazemzadeh holds a PhD in food engineering from Texas A&M University. This is his first book not related to the field of food production. His passion is religious studies and the history of religion. He is currently working on a follow-up volume entitled *Humanity Coming of Age* and a third book on the rationality inherent in the founding principles of the world's great religions. After selling his two food companies, Kay's Naturals and Kay's Processing, he retired to Clara City, Minnesota, where he makes his home with his wife. He has two children and four grandchildren, all of whom live in Minnesota.

Gary Lindberg

Before starting his career in writing and publishing books, Gary Lindberg was an award-winning filmmaker with over a hundred national and international awards. He produced and co-wrote the Paramount feature film *That Was Then, This Is Now* starring Emilio Estevez and Morgan Freeman. Since then, he has authored four #1 bestselling novels and several nonfiction titles. He lives in Minnesota where he has published books for over a hundred authors with his partner at Calumet Editions, Ian Graham Leask.

Made in the USA
Monee, IL
30 September 2023

43678580R00146